篮球记录台人员手册

中国篮球协会　审定

北京体育大学出版社

策划编辑：曾　莉
责任编辑：曾　莉　王泓滢
责任校对：吴海燕
版式设计：李　鹤

图书在版编目（CIP）数据

篮球记录台人员手册 / 中国篮球协会审定. —— 北京:
北京体育大学出版社, 2023.6
　　ISBN 978-7-5644-3846-3

　　Ⅰ. ①篮… Ⅱ. ①中… Ⅲ. ①篮球运动 – 记分法 – 手
册 Ⅳ. ①G841.4-62

中国国家版本馆CIP数据核字(2023)第111973号

篮球记录台人员手册
LANQIU JILUTAI RENYUAN SHOUCE

中国篮球协会　审定

出版发行：	北京体育大学出版社
地　　址：	北京市海淀区农大南路1号院2号楼2层办公B-212
邮　　编：	100084
网　　址：	http://cbs.bsu.edu.cn
发 行 部：	010-62989320
邮 购 部：	北京体育大学出版社读者服务部 010-62989432
印　　刷：	河北盛世彩捷印刷有限公司
开　　本：	880mm×1230mm　　1/32
成品尺寸：	145mm×210mm
印　　张：	8.75
字　　数：	231千字
版　　次：	2023年6月第1版
印　　次：	2023年6月第1次印刷
定　　价：	65.00元

出版说明

- 《篮球记录台人员手册》是中国篮球协会依照国际篮球联合会（简称国际篮联）发布的 *FIBA TABLE OFFICIALS MANUAL v5.0* 翻译和修订的。

- 《篮球记录台人员手册》的翻译和编订力求忠实于原文。如在理解和执行过程中出现争议，以国际篮球联合会官方语言英文版为准。翻译和审校工作可能存在疏漏之处，欢迎广大读者提出意见和建议，以便我们及时修订和完善。

- 本手册王潇凌参与了翻译工作，安一媚参与了编校组织工作。

FOREWORD

FIBA continues its commitment to facilitate and supervise the development of all FIBA family members.

Together with Referees, Referees Instructors and Commissioners, Table Officials are an important part of the Officiating Team family. The role of Table Officials is worldwide crucial in ensuring the smooth running of basketball games.

Modern basketball is constantly evolving in all aspects, in and around the game. Naturally, all the participants must constantly improve their skills and knowledge in order to meet basketball's ever-changing requirements.

The objective of the 5th edition of the FIBA Table Officials' Manual is to upgrade the practical working tool for Table Officials, based on the new FIBA Basketball Rules and Interpretations, valid as of 1st October 2022.

Moreover, the content of this manual has been reviewed since the last edition's release, taking into account the various comments received by Table Officials from all regions.

Same as previously, this Manual is intended to serve FIBA Competitions and National level Competitions alike. We hope it will be helpful and useful in your day-to-day basketball officiating activities.

FIBA Referee Department would like to thank everyone for their contribution and would like to encourage Table Officials to provide profitable feedback in the future. Not only the manual has been updated following the new rules, but some contributions and clips have also been added to improve the understanding of the Table Officials' work.

For any suggestions or if you spot a mistake, please send your comments to refereeing@fiba.basketball.

Thank you for your contribution in striving for excellence in worldwide basketball officiating.

前 言

国际篮联持续致力于促进和监督国际篮联大家庭所有成员的发展。

同裁判员、裁判讲师和技术代表一样，记录台人员是执裁团队的重要组成部分，他们在保障篮球比赛顺利进行的过程中起着至关重要的作用。

现代篮球在赛场内外的各个方面都在不断地发展。顺理成章地，所有的参与者都必须不断提高自身的技能、扩展自己的知识，才能满足篮球不断变化的要求。

国际篮联5.0版记录台人员手册的目标是在最新的国际篮联篮球规则和解释（于2022年10月1日生效）的基础上更新记录台人员的实际工作方法。

此外，在本手册的上一版发布后，我们已对其内容进行了复审，也采纳了部分来自世界各地记录台人员的反馈。

和以往一样，本手册适用于国际篮联比赛和类似规格的国家级比赛。我们希望本手册有助于并有利于您日常与篮球执裁相关的活动。

国际篮联裁判部门感谢大家的贡献，并鼓励记录台人员在今后提供积极的反馈。本手册不仅已根据最新的篮球规则进行了更新，而且在其基础上新增了一些内容和视频，以帮助记录台人员更好地理解他们的工作。

如果您有任何建议或发现任何错误，请将您的建议发送邮件到 refereeing@fiba.basketball。

感谢您为追求卓越的全球篮球执裁工作所作出的贡献。

TABLE OF CONTENTS

目录

Chapter 8

第 1 章
INTRODUCTION
导论

INTRODUCTION

Basketball is a constantly evolving sport. Conceived by Mr. Naismith as an indoor school activity played during the winter, is now played in more than 200 countries. In many of these countries basketball is played at a professional level.

The increasing technical level of teams / leagues must be accompanied by an increase in the technical level of the officiating team (referees and Table Officials), to ensure the smooth running of each game.

An increase in electronic media presence means the work of Table Officials is constantly in the public eye, for example, by showing the running score, the time left to play for a shot.

This Table Officials Manual aims to standardise, unify, and prepare a high-level Table Official.

The Manual is based on new technologies and techniques to help beginners and experienced Table Officials. The use of the video clips will provide for a better understanding of these concepts. At the same time, this Manual is intended as a tool to promote the unification of criteria (method of work, communication, performance standards, signals etc.), for the more experienced Table Officials.

The globalisation of basketball requires the creation of this document to standardise the collaborative dynamics of the Game Officials Team (referees and Table Officials), and to prepare high-level Table Officials for the modern game and competitions. This Manual will promote one methodology for Table Officials in all countries, thus minimising any confusion and maximising consistency.

It is important to adopt the same principles that were used to create other FIBA teaching philosophies, for example, the Mechanics for Referees. The goal is that everybody must "speak" the same basketball language and everybody should "perform" in the same way, regardless of their country.

导论

篮球是一项不断发展的体育运动。这项由奈史密斯先生所创造的适合学校在冬季开展的室内活动，如今已在超过 200 个国家中普及。其中大多数国家也都有着自己的篮球职业联赛。

为了确保每一场比赛的顺利进行，唯有技术水平不断进步的执裁团队（裁判员和记录台人员）才能胜任技术水平日益进步的球队和联赛。

越来越多电子媒体的播报都使公众可以将记录台人员的工作尽收眼底。例如：累积分的显示、一次投篮前剩余时间的显示。

本手册意在使记录台人员的工作标准化、统一化，进而为胜任更高级别的比赛做好准备。

本手册的编制基于最新的科学技术和应用技巧，以同时满足初学者和高水平记录台人员的需求。附带的视频片段也会帮助学习者更好地理解本手册的内容。同时，本手册致力于为高水平记录台人员制定统一的记录台工作标准（工作方法、沟通技巧、执行标准、信号形式等）。

篮球运动的全球化要求为执裁团队（裁判员和记录台人员）建立一套标准化的操作规范以适应动态发展的篮球运动，并以此为现代篮球竞赛储备高水平的记录台人员。本手册为全球各地的记录台人员提供了一套方法论，在最大化减少疑问的同时提高一致性。

重要的是要采用与创建其他国际篮联教学理念相同的原则，例如：裁判法。其目的是要求每一个人，无论来自哪里，都必须在篮球工作中"说"同一种语言和"执行"同一种工作方法。

The mechanics and guidance in the Table Officials Manual are to be understood and followed as fundamental principles in ensuring some uniform and consistent criteria for action, whilst adapting to other cases which do not appear in the Manual. Furthermore, the Manual promotes teamwork among the Table Officials as being a key to success, thus requiring all four Table Officials to work as a seamless and effective team.

ONE GAME – ONE LANGUAGE – ONE METHOD – ONE FIBA

读者应将本手册中所述的工作方法和指导意见作为基本原则去理解和遵守，为的是确保自己能够在面对相同情况时应用一致的尺度，同时也将此原则应用到本手册中未能涵盖的比赛情况中。此外，本手册所推广的团队合作是记录台人员成功完成比赛的关键所在，因此要求由 4 人组成的记录台人员团队必须紧密团结且高效地完成比赛工作。

同一场比赛　同一种语言　同一个方法　同一个FIBA

第 2 章

REFEREES, TABLE OFFICIALS AND COMMISSIONER

裁判员、记录台人员
和技术代表

REFEREES, TABLE OFFICIALS AND COMMISSIONER

2.1 WHO ARE THEY?

The referees shall be a Crew Chief and 2 Umpires. They shall be assisted by the Table Officials and a Commissioner, if present.

The Table Officials shall be the scorer, an assistant scorer, a timer and a shot clock operator. The Table Officials shall sit at the centre of the table on one side of the court, between the team benches. They are responsible for recording the actions that occur during the game and operating the different electronic devices necessary for the proper management of a basketball game.

The Commissioner shall sit between the scorer and the timer. Commissioners primary duty during the game is to supervise the work of the Table Officials and to assist the Crew Chief and Umpires in the smooth running of the game.

- In international FIBA competitions with four Table Officials they will be seated as shown in the photo and diagram below.

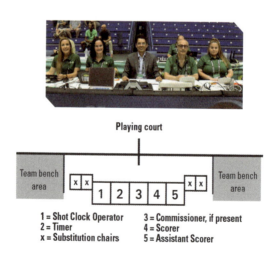

裁判员、记录台人员和技术代表

2.1 他们是谁?

裁判员应是1名主裁判员和2名副裁判员。他们由记录台人员和到场的技术代表协助。

记录台人员应是1名记录员、1名助理记录员、1名计时员和1名进攻计时员。记录台人员应在位于比赛场地一侧、双方球队席之间的记录台中间就座。他们的职责是以记录比赛期间发生的情况和操作不同的电子设备来对篮球比赛进行恰当的管理。

技术代表应坐在记录员和计时员之间。技术代表的主要职责是在比赛期间监督记录台人员的工作以及协助主裁判员和助理裁判员,力求比赛顺利且流畅。

● 国际篮联的比赛应设置4名记录台人员,他们应如下图所示就座。

The Table Officials and their main duties are described below.

Scorer: Recording all actions that occur during the game on the scoresheet.

Timer: Measuring playing time, time-outs and intervals of play.

Shot clock operator: Operating the shot clock and applying the correct shot clock rules.

Assistant scorer: Operating the scoreboard and assisting the scorer.

In the current game of basketball, the responsibility of the Table Official has acquired a growing mportance in the officiating team. However, it must be remembered that they have no executive powers and only the Crew Chief has the power to make final decisions where necessary. The action of the Table Officials must not put either playing team at a disadvantage. Therefore, they must:

- Know the FIBA official rules, interpretations and competition regulations correctly.

- Have a general technical knowledge of refereeing (referees' mechanics on the court, movements, signalling etc.).

- Know exactly what to do in each of the roles indicated above, and in every moment of the game. They should coordinate and help colleagues (be decisive or not procrastinate) so that the table officiating team can act quickly and efficiently.

- Always be good FIBA representatives.

2.2 PERSONAL ATTRIBUTES

There are other qualities that excellent Table Officials should have if they want to avoid putting either team at any disadvantage. These qualities will also ensure that Table Officials are a part of the larger officiating team at a game of basketball.

- **CONCENTRATION:** To successfully perform any task in life, you should be focused and aware of what is happening. Table Officials require a high degree of concentration that must be maintained all through the game.

- **CALM AND SELF-CONTROL:** It is the only way to rationalise situations and resolve any issues that may happen. An excellent Table Official shall strive to set aside a domino effect where a whole series of negative and irrational thoughts lead to a decrease in performance, concentration, and of course, enjoyment.

记录台人员的主要职责如下。

记录员： 在记录表上记录比赛期间发生的所有情况。

计时员： 计量比赛时间、暂停和比赛休息期。

进攻计时员： 操作进攻计时钟，并依照进攻计时钟的规则执行正确的操作。

助理记录员： 操作记录屏，并协助记录员。

现代篮球比赛中，记录台人员的职责在执裁团队中占据着越来越重要的地位。然而，必须牢记的是，记录台人员并没有执行权，只有主裁判员有权在必要时作出最终决定。记录台人员的工作不能将任一队置于不利。因此，他们必须：

- 正确地理解国际篮联篮球规则、篮球规则解释，以及竞赛规定。
- 大致了解执裁技术（场上的裁判法、移动、手势等）。
- 通晓在比赛的任何时间每一个记录台人员的岗位职责。他们应齐心协力，彼此协助（果断，不迟疑），只有这样，记录台人员才能快速和高效地应对比赛。
- 工作中始终以最好的一面代表国际篮联。

2.2 个人属性

除了应避免将任一队置于不利，优秀的记录台人员还应具备一些其他特质。这些特质也将奠定记录台人员在整个执裁团队中的重要地位。

- **专注：** 想要成功地完成生活中的每一项任务，你都应该集中精力并意识到所发生的一切。记录台人员在比赛过程中必须保持精神高度集中。
- **镇定和自控：** 镇定和自控是合理处理场上情况和解决问题的唯一途径。一名优秀的记录台人员应将自身置于"多米诺效应"之外，从而不让负面和非理性的思想影响到自身的工作表现、注意力和愉悦感。

- **TEAM WORK:** Basketball is a team sport. Only by working as a team can the officiating crew perform at their best for the game. No one in the game can be perfect by themselves; we win and lose together as a team. During the game, we help and support each other. If there are any problems during the game, we work together as a team to solve them – not just one person on their own. We should never say: "that is your job and this is mine", because at any time we may need help from our co-officials. Two eyes are not enough to check what is happening on the court. We must use common sense to make the correct decisions at the correct time, working as a team, for the good of the game.

- **ACKNOWLEDGMENT:** If the work of the referee is rarely publicly acknowledged, the work of the table official is even less so. The satisfaction of a job well done; the thanks received from our teammates (other Table Officials and referees); the joy from doing a good job, knowing that each member has contributed to the successful management of the game: this must be enough. Moreover, being a part of the basketball family means that we meet new officiating colleagues, learn from each other and develop long-lasting friendships across many countries. Officiating in basketball is about more than just turning up to a game, doing a job and then going home again.

- **MOTIVATION:** The very best officials are motivated to do the best job that they can in each game, for the benefit of the players and those watching the game. They are also self-motivated, continually working hard to keep up-to-date with changes and to learn from their officiating partners.

- **ASSERTIVENESS:** Assertiveness is a communication skill which is defined as the capacity to acknowledge our own rights while respecting the rights of others, without being manipulated or manipulating others, and without ever being aggressive. The key to a friendly but highly professional approach is often to listen properly and to smile.

- **EMPATHY:** Empathy is the ability to put oneself in someone else's place, emotionally speaking; to imagine how they must be feeling at a particular moment, and to react accordingly. A Table Official must be able to show empathy, and to understand that in some situations, other people might react in a way that is driven by their emotions. We must not take things personally and we must be professional at all times.

- **团队合作**：篮球是一项团队运动。执裁团队只有高效地合作才能以最好的状态服务于比赛。比赛中，没有人能够独善其身，执裁工作的成与败都是团队合作的结果。我们在比赛期间相互协助、彼此支持。我们应协同解决比赛中出现的任何问题，而非让某个个体去独自面对。永远勿言："那是你的工作，这才是我的。"因为我们可能在任何时刻都需要同伴的协助。双眼无法时刻关注场上所发生的一切。我们必须利用常识在正确的时间作出正确的决定，团队协作，为的是更好地完成比赛。

- **认可**：如果裁判员的执裁工作很少有机会能被公众认可，那么记录台人员的工作则更是如此。执裁工作所能带来的职业满足感包括：团队成员对你的感谢（来自其他记录台人员和裁判员）；完成工作的喜悦，清楚地知晓每位裁判员为顺利完成比赛所做出的贡献。职业满足感是十分重要的。更进一步而言，便是融入篮球大家庭并结识更多执裁同仁，在工作中相互学习，以及获得天长地久的跨国友谊。执裁篮球比赛并不仅仅是在做完一项工作后回家这样简单。

- **动力**：最优秀的裁判员会在每场比赛中力求完美，为的是让队员们和观众们都受益。他们通常都会自我激励，并会持续地努力工作，以应对更多的变化，同时向他们的同伴学习。

- **自信**：自信是一种交流技巧，它是一种宣示裁判员权利的能力，同时也是对他人权利的尊重，应当是不卑不亢的。友善和个性化交流的关键在于适时地倾听和微笑。

- **换位思考**：换位思考是一种将自己置身于他人的情感位置中去思考的能力；想象到他人在特定的情境中是如何思考的，同时根据情况作出反应。一名记录台人员必须具备换位思考的能力，并且能够在一些情境中运用这种能力，因为其他人可能会在他们的情绪影响下作出应激反应。我们在遇到情况时，不能感情用事，必须全程保持职业态度。

- **HUMILITY AND RESPECT:** The task of the Table Official is not the same as that of the referee. It does not matter how old we are, how much experience we have or how well qualified we are. We all play an equal part in the officiating team. We must never consider ourselves superior or inferior to our co-officials. At the same time, we must have the same respect for our co-officials as we have for all those who participate in the game.

2.3 BEHAVIOUR – CODE OF CONDUCT

Any person who plays a role within the officiating team must have an ability to relate to their co-officials. There are other groups of people that Table Officials must also be able to relate to. In the context of a basketball game, from the time the Table Officials arrive at the arena until they leave after the game, they will relate to different people as follows:

- **FANS AND TEAM MEMBERS:** We must be professional and neutral at all times. We should not engage in excessive conversation, especially if someone or a team express a grievance. We must not show, either in our actions or in our conversations, any bias for one group over another. This includes our use of social media.

- **PLAYERS AND COACHES:** We need to use our empathy in these situations. Coaches and players may be unkind or aggressive towards us, but we must behave professionally about this. We must not be aggressive or threatening in responding to these situations; we must remain calm and focused. Where appropriate, and at the right time, Table Officials should talk to the referees discreetly about any behaviour that concerns them.

- **谦逊与尊重**：记录台人员的工作与裁判员的工作并不完全一致。这与年龄无关，与资历无关，与获得的认证无关。执裁团队中的每个人都是平等的。永远不要认为自己高人一等，也不要认为自己技不如人。同时，我们应当对参与执裁的每一位同仁保持应有的尊重。

2.3 行为规范

执裁团队中的每个成员都必须具备与他人协作的能力。记录台人员还要具备与其他人员交流的能力。在一场篮球比赛中，记录台人员从到达场馆到离开场馆，都要在与他人的沟通与交流中牢记以下准则：

- **面对观众与球队成员**：我们必须始终保持专业和中立。切记不能与他们过多地交谈，尤其是当有人或有球队表现出不满的时候。在与他们进行的行为和谈话中，我们不能表现出对其中一方的偏袒。这同样也包括我们使用社交媒体的过程。
- **面对队员和教练员**：在这些情况下，我们需要运用自己的换位思考能力。教练员和队员可能会对我们表现出不友好甚至愤怒，但我们必须以职业化的态度应对这些情况。我们不能以愤怒甚至威胁的态度作出回应，我们必须时刻保持冷静和专注。当有合适的时机，记录台人员应当谨慎地向裁判员讲述他们遭遇的情况。

- **THEIR CO-OFFICIALS:** There must be mutual respect, collaboration, a sense of team, and an acceptance of each role that has been assigned. If we need to call the attention of the referees about something that has occurred on or off the court, we should do this discreetly to avoid putting them in a difficult situation.

● **他们的同伴：**记录台人员在与同伴的交流中，必须相互尊重，
积极合作，具备团队意识，以及认同对于每个角色的任务分配。
如果我们需要就场上或场下的有关事宜引起裁判员的注意时，
我们应当谨慎地进行沟通，以避免将裁判员置于不利的境地。

第 3 章

TABLE OFFICIALS COMMON DUTIES

记录台人员的主要职责

TABLE OFFICIALS COMMON DUTIES

3.1 NOMINATION

The pre-game begins when a table official receives the nomination for the game. At this time, you should commence your preparation by analysing your journey options to the arena and understanding who will be your teammates, the importance of the game (age, category, regular season or play-off, etc.), checking and ensuring that you have all the necessary equipment and uniform prepared well before the day you travel.

3.2 ARRIVAL AT THE VENUE

It is essential that all Table Officials make their travel arrangements to arrive at their destination in good time. Punctuality is an essential aspect of the officiating team.

- In FIBA competitions, all officials are required to arrive at the arena at least 90 minutes before the game is scheduled to begin.

- You should plan the journey well in advance, anticipating things such as traffic congestion, bad weather conditions and so on. This is especially important if you have not been to the arena before.

- It is important to bring a list with the telephone numbers of your co-officials, to notify them of any unexpected delays.

- On arriving at the venue, you should let the organisers and the Commissioner (if present) know that you have arrived. You should then meet with the rest of the officiating team.

记录台人员的主要职责

3.1 选派

赛前阶段开始于记录台人员收到选派通知。此时，你应当着手准备：规划前往场馆的行程、知悉与你搭档的同伴、了解比赛的重要程度（年龄、组别、常规赛或季后赛等）、启程前检查和确认所有必要的设备和制服。

3.2 抵达场馆

所有的记录台人员必须安排好自己的行程，以确保在规定时间内到达目的地。守时是执裁团队最基本的素质之一。

- 国际篮联要求所有记录台人员必须至少在规定的比赛开始时间前 90 分钟到达场馆。
- 你应当提前规划行程，以应对可能出现的意外状况，例如：交通拥堵、恶劣天气等。如果你未曾去过将要去的那个场馆，提前规划就显得更为重要了。

- 携带一份执裁团队的通讯录是非常重要的，这样可以及时告知他们可能意外发生的延误。
- 到达场馆后，你应当向赛事组织方和到场的技术代表报道。然后你应当与已经到达的执裁团队会面。

3.3 DRESS CODE

Personal appearance is very important. Table Officials should take care of their image, maintaining a professional appearance in themselves and their work; thus, obtaining respect from all.

Remember that you, like the referees, are a representative on court of your leagues, federations, and country.

Your words, your attire and your behaviour will be observed attentively by all participants.

Table Officials should arrive at the venue in smart business clothing and be prepared to change into their table officiating uniform. Table Officials should change at the end of the game and leave the venue in smart business clothing.

It is not acceptable to go to the venues wearing sportswear, shorts and sports shoes. You must take care of your appearance, ensuring you are clean and tidy, including your hair and facial hair.

The Table Officials' uniform should be in good condition, clean and properly ironed.

3.4 TABLE OFFICIALS' MEETING

It is important for the Table Officials team to have a talk and prepare properly for the game in a pre-game meeting.

This will form a strong team. It should take place in your designated room and away from other people at the arena.

In the pregame meeting, you should discuss at least the following points:

- Confirmed game start time.

- Recent changes in rules and interpretations.

- Game context: level of difficulty, external and internal factors of the game, situation in the league (regular season, finals, play-offs, etc.). This means officiating all games with equal seriousness, regardless of their status.

3.3 着装要求

个人形象是很重要的。记录台人员应当关注他们的自身形象，以维护其个人和执裁工作的专业形象，并且从中获得尊重。

请牢记，如同裁判员一样，你们在场上所代表的是你们的联赛、协会和国家。

你的一言一行、你的穿着打扮和你的行为将会被所有的参与者看到并记住。

记录台人员应穿着商务便服前往场馆，然后再换上记录台人员的制服。记录台人员应在比赛结束后换回商务便服，然后再离开场馆。

穿着运动服、短裤和运动鞋前往场馆是不可接受的。你必须时刻关注自身形象，确保着装整洁，包括打理自己的头发和胡须。

记录台人员的制服必须保持完好、整洁，并且是被熨烫过的。

3.4 记录台人员的会议

记录台人员在赛前会上进行交流和赛前准备是十分重要的。

赛前准备会可以促成一个强而有力的团队。赛前准备会应当在指定的空间内进行，且该空间应当远离场馆内的其他人员。

在赛前准备会中，你们至少应当就如下问题进行交流：

- 确认比赛的开始时间。
- 篮球规则和篮球规则解释的最新改动。
- 比赛属性：难度级别、比赛的外在和内在影响因素、联赛的情况（常规赛、总决赛、季后赛等）。这意味着执裁所有的比赛必须以同样严肃的态度面对，无论这些比赛处于什么样的状态。

- Coordination of the procedures to follow in different critical situations: baskets scored, time-outs, substitutions, end of the quarter/game, change in team in control of the ball, team fouls, alternating possession procedure, etc.

- Special considerations about this arena: location of the game/shot clocks, what to do in special conditions or malfunctions, team benches, when to do a full check of all devices.

- Eye contact.

- Communication methods with the referees and the other Table Officials, including communication in unexpected situations.

- How to solve any problems that might arise.

- Special conditions for the game such as TV time-outs, minute of silence, presentations, tributes, etc.

- During the half-time, the Table Officials can leave the table and have to come back 5 minutes before the beginning of the 2nd half-time. But there should always be one of them staying at the table to watch the teams.

- 根据比赛的进程而团结协作以应对任何不同的重要情况：中篮分值、暂停、替换、一节或比赛的结束、球队控制球权的转换、球队犯规、交替拥有程序等。
- 须对比赛场馆特别考虑之处：比赛计时钟和进攻计时钟的位置、在特殊情况和故障情况下的应对措施、球队席区域、何时对所有设备进行充分检查。
- 眼神交流。

- 与裁判员和记录台人员的交流方法，包括应对意外情况的交流。
- 如何解决可能发生的问题。
- 比赛的特殊规定，例如：媒体暂停、默哀、展示活动、致敬活动等。
- 在中场比赛休息期间，记录台人员可以离开记录台，但必须在下半时比赛开始之前 5 分钟回到记录台。但是，记录台上始终应有 1 位记录台人员就座并观察比赛。

3.5 PRE-GAME DUTIES

- Identify the Technical Delegate, Commissioner, or court manager of the game (if any).

- Check the table equipment and electronic devices (game clock, shot clock, acoustic signals and electronic scoreboard), and share any unusual features with your co-officials .

- Request the team lists: each team must give its own list at least 40 minutes before the game is scheduled to begin.

- Notify the Commissioner (if present) or the Crew Chief of any potential issues with the team lists or any other documentation needed to play the game.

- Prepare the scoresheet according to the rules. In the case of a FIBA Digital Scoresheet (DSS), the prepared scoresheet should be printed out at least 20 minutes before the scheduled tip off for the game.

- Table Officials must be at the table before the referees enter the court.

- Keep the game ball safe and secure.

- Measure the 20 minute interval of play before the start of the game (with the referees present on court). In the event of team presentations, the timer will inform the referees when 7, 8, or 9 minutes (the Local Organising Committee (LOC) will generally decide this), remain prior to the start of the game, depending on whether national anthems must be played. In any case, the timer will stop the clock when 3 minutes remain until the start of the game, if the presentation is not finished. In the event of a minute of silence being observed, this is done just before the start of the game, with the starting players on the court.

- Assist in checking how many people are seated in the team bench areas.

3.5 赛前职责

- 识别技术代表或赛场管理员（如有的话）。

- 检查记录台设备和电子设备（比赛计时钟、进攻计时钟、声音信号、电子记录屏），如果这些设备具备任何不常见的特性，则应与同伴分享这些信息。

- 索要球队参赛名单：每支参赛球队必须至少在比赛开始前 40 分钟提交参赛名单。

- 如球队的参赛名单或是任何与本场比赛相关的文件存在可能的问题，应告知到场的技术代表或主裁判员。

- 根据规则准备记录表。如使用国际篮联电子记录表（DSS），则必须至少在跳球时间之前 20 分钟进行打印。

- 记录台人员必须在裁判员入场前就位。

- 确保比赛用球的安全可靠。

- 赛前 20 分钟开始比赛休息期间的倒计时（裁判员须到达赛场）。在有球队入场仪式的比赛中，计时员要在赛前 7 分钟、8 分钟或 9 分钟时（通常由赛事组委会决定具体时间）提示裁判员，具体时间取决于是否需要播放国歌。在任何情况下，如果入场仪式没有完毕，计时员要在赛前 3 分钟时停止计时钟。在默哀 1 分钟的情况下，该活动应在比赛之前完成，届时首发队员需要站在场上。

- 协助检查双方球队席区域就座的人数。

- The shot clock operator will run the shot clock down when the referees are present on court so that they can hear the sound of the device when a shot clock period expires.

- If a whistle-controlled time system is used, the timer has to check that it works well also with the referees on the court, before the game starts.

- Request from the head coach of each team confirmation of the names and corresponding numbers of their team members, the names of the head coach and first assistant coach and the starting 5 players and get the head coach to sign the scoresheet. This should be done at least 10 minutes before the beginning of the game (Team A head coach first, then Team B). The scorer will share this information with the statisticians and court announcer, if present.

- The timer will sound the signal 3' before the start of the game and then again 1'30" before the start of the game. The referee will indicate 3' by showing three fingers in the usual manner and then will blow the whistle when 1'30" remain to indicate to the teams that they are to go to their own team bench areas.

3.6 DUTIES DURING THE GAME

- Maintain high levels of concentration, particularly towards the end of quarters of play and in the final two minutes of the game.

- Apply the rules correctly.

- Collaborate with table co-officials and referees.

- Speak professionally with the members of both playing teams.

- Table Officials should watch the flow of the game carefully, anticipating possible requests for substitutions and time-outs, paying special attention to time-out requests after scored baskets.

- Remember that the Table Officials must be discreet in the use of acoustic signals. In exceptional cases the whistle can be used in certain situations to attract the attention of the referees.

- Do not ever put the referees in a no-win situation. Table officials must know exactly what happened before they call the referee to the table to report any actions by bench personnel.

- It is strictly forbidden to make any signals that can compromise the decisions of the referees.

- Give information and support to any member of the officiating team who requests it, but in a discreet way.

- 当裁判员进入比赛场地后，进攻计时员应当开动进攻计时钟，以使裁判员可以听到进攻计时钟的声音信号。
- 如使用哨声控制计时系统，计时员必须在比赛开始前检查该设备并确保该设备可以被裁判员正常使用。
- 向主教练确认参赛队员名单和号码、主教练和第一助理教练的姓名，确认 5 名首发队员，并让主教练在记录表上签字。这些应当至少在比赛开始前 10 分钟完成（主队为先，客队随后）。记录员应向到场的技术统计员和宣告员传达这些信息。
- 计时员在比赛前 3 分钟发出信号，然后在赛前 1 分 30 秒再次发出信号。主裁判员在赛前 3 分钟时鸣哨，并且以常用的伸出 3 根手指的手势提示；在赛前 1 分 30 秒再次鸣哨，并提示双方球队返回各自球队席区域。

3.6 赛中职责

- 保持高度专注，特别是在一节的结束和比赛的最后 2 分钟阶段。
- 正确地应用规则。
- 积极与其他记录台人员和裁判员合作。
- 与双方球队人员的交流体现职业化。
- 记录台人员应当仔细地观察比赛进程，预测可能出现的替换和暂停，特别要关注中篮之后请求暂停的情况。
- 请牢记，记录台人员在使用声音信号时必须格外严谨。在特殊情况下，使用口哨同样可以引起裁判员的注意。
- 永远不要将裁判员置于不利的情况。记录台人员在叫裁判员到记录台听取有关球队席人员的情况汇报之前必须清楚地知道究竟发生了什么。
- 禁止记录台人员发出可能对裁判员的决定产生干扰的信号。
- 当执裁团队的任一成员向你索取信息或协助时，给予严谨的回复。

- Clarify the procedure if a request by the referees is made following an unclear situation (end of a quarter, goal made etc.). Never use a gesture or speak loudly. Only give information if the referee requests it, and assign only one speaker from the Table Officials crew.

- Record separately the minutes and the participants in fouls.

- Procedures during a fight and / or team bench personnel leaving the bench area. Should a fight break out on court, and / or the team bench personnel leave the bench area, the Table Officials must remain focused. The assistant scorer must observe the visiting team bench, the shot clock operator the local team bench and the scorer and the timer must observe the playing court. They are to note the events unfolding on court and in the team bench areas, recording any actions of players, coaches and team followers, in order to assist the referees and Commissioner.

- Inform the referees about any malfunction of the devices whenever the rules provide the opportunity.

3.7 POST-GAME DUTIES

- Avoid discussions or comments with any non-member of the officiating team.

- The scorer should complete the scoresheet as indicated in the rules and in this Manual.

- Observe and record any incident that occurred after the end of the game.

- Help the referees to write a report to the organising body of the competition, if they need assistance.

- 明确当裁判员提出需要澄清模糊情况（一节的结束、中篮有效等）时的流程。绝对不要使用肢体语言或大声喧哗。只有当裁判员提出请求时才提供相应信息，并且在记录台人员中确认唯一一名负责沟通信息的人员。
- 分别记录发生犯规的时间（分钟）和人员。
- 打架和／或球队席人员离开球队席区域的处理流程：当场上发生了一起打架情况和／或球队席人员离开球队席区域时，记录台人员必须保持专注。助理记录员必须观察客队球队席，进攻计时员必须观察主队球队席，记录员和计时员则必须观察比赛场地。他们应当记录场上和球队席的事件始末，记录关于队员、教练员和球队席人员的任何违犯行为，以协助裁判员和技术代表的工作。
- 无论按照规则而言是否出现了停止比赛的机会，当设备发生故障时应立即通知裁判员。

3.7 赛后职责

- 避免与任何非执裁团队人员进行交谈或发表评论。
- 记录员应当根据规则和本手册的规定完成记录表的填写。
- 观察和记录比赛结束后发生的任何特别情况。
- 当裁判员需要协助时，帮助他们为赛事组织机构书写报告。

- Check (print in the case of the DSS) the scoresheet and sign before giving it for final approval and signature by the referee.

- Procedure in case of protest. If a team decides to file the protest, they must follow the procedure described in the FIBA Official Basketball Rules. Teams as well as referees, Technical Delegate/Commissioner and Table Officials must comply with the timeline requirements related to the protest procedure. Immediately after the end of the game, the scorer must indicate in the column "The game ended at" the exact time when the game has ended. The referees must not rush to sign the scoresheet. Instead, the Crew Chief together with the Technical Delegate/Commissioner shall verify that that the scorer has entered the time in the "Game ended" column. The referees shall then go to their dressing room and wait for the allocated 15 minutes after the end of the game.

  The Table Officials and the Technical Delegate/ Commissioner shall not leave the scorer's table during the 15 minutes after the end of the game. Once the team captain signs the scoresheet in the column "Captain's signature in case of protest", the scorer and the FIBA Technical Delegate/Commissioner shall go the referees' dressing room and present the scoresheet to the Crew Chief. After the verification of the scoresheet, the Crew Chief shall sign the scoresheet, write down the captain signature time, and the FIBA Technical Delegate/Commissioner will distribute the copies of the scoresheet to both teams.

  The protesting team, however, must submit in writing the reasons for the protest no later than 1 hour following the end of the game. The FIBA Technical Delegate/Commissioner, the referees and the Table Officials must stay in the sport hall at least 1 hour and under no circumstances may they leave the sport hall until all the paperwork is finalised and the confirmation of the completed procedure has been received from FIBA / FIBA Regional Office. The Crew Chief must report in writing the incident which led to the protest and submit it to the FIBA Technical Delegate / Commissioner and the respective FIBA Regional Office.

- Give back to the teams a copy of the scoresheet and any license cards or other documents.

- Ask the referee, the Technical Delegate or the Commissioner (if present) for permission to leave the arena.

- Use the post-game meeting in the changing area to ask about any situations in the game where a misunderstanding took place, or where any unusual situations happened.

- 将记录表递交裁判员核查和签字前（如果是电子记录表，则在打印前），检查记录表的填写情况。

- 申诉程序。如果有球队决定提交申诉，他们必须遵守国际篮联篮球规则的申诉程序。执裁团队、技术代表和记录台人员必须遵守申诉程序的时间限定。比赛结束后，记录员应当立即在"比赛结束时间"一栏中填入比赛结束的准确时间。裁判员不能急于在记录表上签字。相反，主裁判员应当与技术代表一起核实记录员填入的比赛结束时间。随后，裁判员应回到更衣室，按申诉程序规定等候 15 分钟。

  记录台人员与技术代表，应当在比赛结束后的 15 分钟内，继续在记录台等待。一旦球队队长在记录表"申诉队长签字"一栏中签上名字，记录员与国际篮联技术代表应当到裁判员更衣室，向主裁判员呈现记录表的情况。主裁判员应在核实记录表之后在记录表上签字，并记录申诉队长签字的时间，国际篮联技术代表应向双方球队分发记录表的副页。

  提出申诉申请的球队，必须在比赛结束后的 1 小时之内提交书面申请，并说明提出申诉的原因。国际篮联技术代表、裁判员和记录台人员必须在体育馆内等待至少 1 小时，他们不得在书面申请已经提交完成，并且国际篮联或国际篮联洲际办公室确认已经收到这些文件之前离开体育馆。主裁判员必须完成书面报告，在报告中说明球队申诉事件的情况，并且将其提交给国际篮联技术代表和对应的国际篮联洲际办公室。

- 归还球队申诉所使用的记录表、证件和相关文件。

- 请示裁判员或到场的技术代表，是否可以离开体育馆。

- 在一个独立的更衣室内召开赛后总结会，询问比赛中发生了哪些误解，以及发生了哪些不常见的状况。

PROTEST PROCEDURE

1. A team may file a protest if its interests have been adversely affected by:

   a. an error in scorekeeping, time-keeping or shot clock operations, which was not corrected by the officials.

   b. a decision to forfeit, cancel, postpone, not resume or not play the game.

   c. a violation of the applicable eligibility rules.

2. In order to be admissible, a protest shall comply with the following procedure:

   a. The captain (CAP) of that team shall, no later than 15 minutes following the end of the game, inform the Crew Chief that the team is protesting against the result of the game and sign the scoresheet in the 'Captain's signature in case of protest' column.

   b. The team shall submit the protest reasons in writing no later than 1 hour following the end of the game.

   c. A fee of CHF 1,500 shall be applied to each protest and shall be paid in case the protest is rejected.

3. The Crew Chief shall, following receipt of the protest reasons, report the incident which leads to the protest to the FIBA representative or the competent body in writing.

4. The competent body shall issue any procedural requests which it deems appropriate and shall decide on the protest as soon as possible, and in any case no later than 24 hours following the end of the game. The competent body shall use any reliable evidence and can take any appropriate decision, including, without limitation, partial or full replay of the game. The competent body may not decide to change the result of the game unless there is clear and conclusive evidence that, had it not been for the error that gave rise to the protest, the new result would have certainly materialised.

5. The decision of the competent body is also considered as a field of play rule decision and is not subject to further review or appeal. Exceptionally, decisions on eligibility may be appealed as provided for in the applicable regulations.

6. Special rules for FIBA competitions or competitions which do not provide otherwise in their regulations:

   a. In case the competition is in tournament format, the competent body for all protests shall be the Technical Committee (see FIBA Internal Regulations, Book 2).

申诉程序

1. 如果某球队认为下列情况已对该队造成不利，可以提出申诉：

    a. 记录、计时或进攻计时钟出现错误，且没有被裁判员纠正。

    b. 弃权、取消、延期、不恢复或不进行比赛的决定。

    c. 违反所适用的球员资格规定的行为。

2. 为了使该申诉被接受，应遵从下列程序：

    a. 该队队长（CAP）应在比赛结束后 15 分钟内通知主裁判员，该队对比赛的结果提出申诉，并在记录表上标示"球队申诉队长签名"的栏内签字。

    b. 该队应在比赛结束后 1 小时内提交申诉原因的书面文件给主裁判员。

    c. 每次申诉应支付 1500 瑞士法郎的费用，如申诉被拒绝，该费用将不予退回。

3. 主裁判员在收到申诉原因的文件后，应用书面报告向国际篮联的代表或主管机构陈述导致该申诉的事件情况。

4. 主管机构应启用他们所认为恰当的受诉程序，并应立刻对该申诉作出裁决；无论如何，该裁决的作出时间不应超过该场比赛结束后的 24 小时。主管机构应使用一切可靠的证据，包括并不限于使用部分或全部的比赛重放，来作出恰当的裁决。除非有清晰确凿的证据证明申诉文件所述的原因定会导致比赛结果的不同，不然主管机构不会作出更改比赛结果的裁决。

5. 主管机构的裁决也被认为是该赛事仲裁的最终决定，不接受进一步的审查或上诉。在例外情况下，对有关资格问题的裁决可根据适用的条例规定提出上诉。

6. 国际篮联的比赛或其规程中未做其他规定的比赛的特别规则：

    a. 如果是联赛形式的比赛，则接受所有申诉的主管机构应是技术委员会（见国际篮联的内部章程，第 2 册）。

b. In case of home and away games, the competent body for protests relating to eligibility issues shall be the FIBA Disciplinary Panel. For all other issues giving rise to a protest, the competent body shall be FIBA acting through one or more persons with expertise on the implementation and interpretation of the Official Basketball Rules (see FIBA Internal Regulations, Book 2).

b. 如果是主客场赛制的比赛，接受与资格问题有关的申诉的主管机构应是国际篮联纪律委员会。对于所有其他引起申诉的问题，主管机构应由国际篮联组织一名或多名对国际篮联篮球规则的实践和解释有专长的人士组成（见国际篮联的内部章程，第 2 册）。

PROTEST PROCEDURE CHECKLIST					
GAME PARTICIPANTS INVOLVED					
PROTESTING TEAM	OPPONENT TEAM	REFEREES	TECHNICAL DELEGATE OR COMMISSIONER	TABLE OFFICIALS	COMPETENT BODY
END OF GAME					
The captain signs in the scoresheet no later than 15 minutes after the end of the game.		Immediately after the end of the game the Crew Chief verifies that the scorer enters the time in the 'Game ended' column. Referees go to the dressing room.	Technical Delegate (TD) or Commissioner (COM) verifies that the scorer enters the time in the 'Game ended' column. TD or COM remains at the scorer's table.	The scorer enters the time in the 'Game ended' column. Table Officials remain at the scorer's table until the Crew Chief gives them permission to leave.	
15 MIN AFTER END OF GAME					
No later than 1 hour following the end of the game the team submits the protest reason(s) in writing to the TD or COM.	The opponent team receives the copy of the scoresheet.	Crew Chief verifies and signs the scoresheet.	Following the Crew Chief's signature, the TD or COM distribute the copies of the scoresheet to both teams.	The scorer brings the scoresheet to the referees' dressing room for verification and signature. Table officials still remain in the sport hall until the Crew Chief or TD/COM give them permission to leave.	
1 HOUR AFTER END OF GAME					
If the written report is not submitted within 1 hour following the end of the game the protest shall be considered withdrawn.	TD or COM inform the team whether the opponent team submits the written report or the protest is withdrawn.	Following the receipt of the protest reasons, the Crew Chief shall send the written report to the competent body.	Following the receipt of the protest reasons, the TD or COM shall send the written report to the competent body OR note on the score-sheet and in their report that the protest was considered withdrawn.	Table Officials' involvement in the game ends.	It may ask for additional information from all game participants: teams, referees, TD or COM, Table Officials.
24 HOURS AFTER END OF GAME					
Team is informed regarding the decision of the competent body.	Team is informed regarding the decision of the competent body.				It issues the decision no later than 24 hours following the end of the game.

TIMELINE

申诉程序备忘录					
所涉及的比赛参与者					
申诉队	对方队	裁判员	技术代表	记录台人员	竞赛的组织部门
比赛结束时					
队长应在比赛结束后15分钟内在记录表上签字。		主裁判员应在比赛结束后立刻核实记录员在"比赛结束时间"栏内填入时间。裁判员应回到更衣室。	技术代表应核实记录员在"比赛结束时间"栏内填入时间。技术代表应留在记录台。	记录员在"比赛结束时间"栏内填入时间。在主裁判员允许记录台人员离开之前，他们应留在记录台。	
比赛结束后15分钟					
该队应在比赛结束后1小时内提交申诉原因的书面文件给技术代表。	对方队得到一份记录表的副页。	主裁判员核实并在记录表上签字。	主裁判员在记录表上签字后，技术代表应向双方球队分发记录表的副页。	记录员将记录表带去裁判员更衣室，以供裁判员核实和签字。在主裁判员或技术代表允许记录台人员离开之前，他们应留在体育馆内。	
比赛结束后1小时					
如果该队在比赛结束后1小时内未提交申诉原因的书面文件，则视其撤销申诉。	技术代表应告知对方队申诉队是否提交了申诉原因的书面文件。	在收到申诉原因的书面文件后，主裁判员应向主管机构提交书面报告。	在收到申诉原因的书面文件后，技术代表应向主管机构提交书面报告，或在记录表上注明以及在报告中写明申诉已撤销。	本场比赛的记录台人员工作结束。	可能会向比赛参与者(球队、裁判员、技术代表、记录台人员)询问更多信息。
比赛结束后24小时					
将主管机构作出的裁决通知球队。	将主管机构作出的裁决通知球队。				该裁决的作出时间不应超过该场比赛结束后的24小时。

第 4 章
THE SCORER
记录员

THE SCORER

4.1 SCORER'S DUTIES

The scorer shall keep a record of:

- **Teams**, by entering the names and numbers of the players who are to start the game and of all substitutes who enter the game. When there is an infraction of the rules regarding the five players to start the game, substitutions or numbers of players, the nearest referee should be notified as soon as possible.
- **Running summary of points scored**, by entering the field goals and the free throws made.
- **Fouls charged**. The scorer shall record the technical fouls charged against each head coach (2 'C 'or 2 'B'+'C') and must notify the referees immediately when a head coach should be disqualified. Similarly, the referees must be notified immediately when a player has committed 2 unsportsmanlike or technical fouls or 1 technical foul and 1 unsportsmanlike foul (a combination) and should be disqualified.
- **Time-outs**. The scorer shall notify the head coach through a referee when the head coach has no more time-outs left in a half or overtime.
- **The next alternating possession**, by operating the alternating possession arrow. The scorer shall reverse the direction of the alternating possession arrow immediately after the end of the first half as the teams shall exchange baskets for the second half.
- **Head coach's challenge** confirmed by the referees. The scorer shall inform the referees when a head coach requests erroneously a challenge for the second time.

记录员

4.1 记录员的职责

记录员应当记录以下信息:

- **球队**:填写参加比赛的队员姓名和号码,并且在替补队员上场时进行记录。当出现 5 名首发队员违犯规则、违规替换或号码问题时,记录员应当尽快提醒就近的裁判员。

- **记录累积分**:根据场上中篮和罚球的分值记录累积分。

- **登记犯规**:记录员应登记主教练的技术犯规(2 个 "C" 或 2 个 "B" +1 个 "C"),并必须在一名主教练应被取消比赛资格时立即通知裁判员。与之类似,记录员还应在一名队员被宣判 2 次违反体育精神的犯规,或 2 次技术犯规,或 1 次技术犯规和 1 次违反体育精神的犯规组合时,立即通知裁判员该队员应被取消比赛资格。

- **暂停**:在任一半时或决胜期,当某队已经没有暂停机会时,记录员应通过裁判员通知该队主教练。

- **下一次的交替拥有球权**:通过操作交替拥有箭头,指示下一次交替拥有的球权。因为第一个半时结束后,双方球队应在第二个半时交换场地,所以记录员应在第一个半时结束时,立即翻转交替拥有箭头。

- **主教练挑战**:经裁判员确认的主教练挑战。如果一名主教练第二次错误地请求了挑战,记录员应立刻通知裁判员。

4.2 SCORER'S EQUIPMENT AND NECESSARY MATERIALS

For the game, the scorer must have the following equipment.

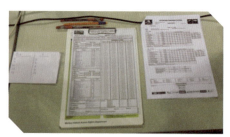

From the local team or organisation:

- Scoresheet or a computer with DSS.
- Alternating possession arrow.

In addition, the following are required:

- Dark pens (blue or black) and red pens.
- A ruler.
- A whistle (for special cases).
- Spare scoresheets (regardless of LOC or home team duties).
- Notice paper to take note of incidents (can be useful if required to make a report to the organising body of the competition), alternating possession arrow changes and players on the court.
- Clips to attach the scoresheet to a clip board, if necessary.

It is also mandatory that the scorer brings the rulebook, interpretations and the Table Officials Manua in paper or digital format.

4.3 THE OFFICIAL SCORESHEET

The scoresheet is the official record of the game. The information contained shall reflect the activities of the game.

The scoresheet keeps a record of the teams, running summary of points scored, fouls charged against each player and coach, and time-outs granted.

After the game, the teams receive a copy of the original, so they have an official document which records the important actions of the game.

The scorer is the main Table Official responsible for recording the actions of the game on the scoresheet, according to the rules. The scorer should write neatly and clearly to ensure high readability of this official document.

4.2 所需的设备和必要的材料

比赛中，必须为记录员配
备以下设备。

主队或组织方应提供：

- 记录表或配备电子记录
  表的电脑。
- 交替拥有箭头。

除此之外，还应为记录员
配备：

- 深色笔（蓝色或黑色）和红色笔。
- 一把尺子。
- 一个口哨（发生特殊情况时使用）。
- 额外的记录表（当地组织方或主队的责任）。
- 记录用纸，用来记录特别情况（为完成提交赛事组织者的书面
  报告使用）、交替拥有箭头变换次序，以及队员的上场信息。
- 文件夹，如有必要可用以夹住记录表。

同时，比赛要求记录员随身携带篮球规则、篮球规则解释和篮球记
录台人员手册的纸质版或电子版文件。

4.3 官方的记录表

记录表是篮球比赛的官方记录。表中包含的信息应能够反映比赛
中发生的情况。

记录表中所登记的信息应包括双方球队的累积分、每名队员和教
练员的犯规次数，以及被准予的暂停。

比赛结束后，应给予球队一份原始记录表的复印件，以便他们通
过官方记录而获取重要比赛的信息。

记录员是记录台人员中负责根据规则在记录表上记录比赛过程的
人员。记录员应当整洁和清晰地填写记录表，以确保其作为官方文件
的高可读性。

FEDERATION INTERNATIONALE DE BASKETBALL
INTERNATIONAL BASKETBALL FEDERATION
SCORESHEET

Team A _____ Team B _____

| Competition _____ | Date _____ | Time _____ | Crew chief _____ |
| Game No. _____ | Place _____ | Umpire 1 _____ | Umpire 2 _____ |

Team A _____

Time-outs

H1	☐☐	Q1 1 2 3 4	Q2 1 2 3 4
H2	☐☐	Q3 1 2 3 4	Q4 1 2 3 4
OT	☐☐	HCC ☐	

Team fouls

Licence no.	Players	No.	Player in	Fouls 1 2 3 4 5

Head coach _____
First assistant coach _____

Team B _____

Time-outs

H1	☐☐	Q1 1 2 3 4	Q2 1 2 3 4
H2	☐☐	Q3 1 2 3 4	Q4 1 2 3 4
OT	☐☐	HCC ☐	

Team fouls

Licence no.	Players	No.	Player in	Fouls 1 2 3 4 5

Head coach _____
First assistant coach _____

RUNNING SCORE

A	B		A	B		A	B		A	B
1	1		41	41		81	81		121	121
2	2		42	42		82	82		122	122
3	3		43	43		83	83		123	123
4	4		44	44		84	84		124	124
5	5		45	45		85	85		125	125
6	6		46	46		86	86		126	126
7	7		47	47		87	87		127	127
8	8		48	48		88	88		128	128
9	9		49	49		89	89		129	129
10	10		50	50		90	90		130	130
11	11		51	51		91	91		131	131
12	12		52	52		92	92		132	132
13	13		53	53		93	93		133	133
14	14		54	54		94	94		134	134
15	15		55	55		95	95		135	135
16	16		56	56		96	96		136	136
17	17		57	57		97	97		137	137
18	18		58	58		98	98		138	138
19	19		59	59		99	99		139	139
20	20		60	60		100	100		140	140
21	21		61	61		101	101		141	141
22	22		62	62		102	102		142	142
23	23		63	63		103	103		143	143
24	24		64	64		104	104		144	144
25	25		65	65		105	105		145	145
26	26		66	66		106	106		146	146
27	27		67	67		107	107		147	147
28	28		68	68		108	108		148	148
29	29		69	69		109	109		149	149
30	30		70	70		110	110		150	150
31	31		71	71		111	111		151	151
32	32		72	72		112	112		152	152
33	33		73	73		113	113		153	153
34	34		74	74		114	114		154	154
35	35		75	75		115	115		155	155
36	36		76	76		116	116		156	156
37	37		77	77		117	117		157	157
38	38		78	78		118	118		158	158
39	39		79	79		119	119		159	159
40	40		80	80		120	120		160	160

Scores

Quarter ①	A _____	B _____
Quarter ②	A _____	B _____
Quarter ③	A _____	B _____
Quarter ④	A _____	B _____
Overtimes	A _____	B _____

Final Score Team A _____ Team B _____

Name of winning team _____

Game ended at (hh:mm) _____

Scorer _____
Assistant scorer _____
Timer _____
Shot clock operator _____

Crew Chief _____
Umpire 1 _____ Umpire 2 _____
Captain's signature in case of protest _____

Diagram9   Scoresheet

国际篮球联合会记录表

A队 _____ B队 _____

竞赛名称 _____ 日期 _____ 时间 _____ 主裁判员 _____
比赛序号 _____ 地点 _____ 副裁判员1 _____ 副裁判员2 _____

A队

暂停		全队犯规
上半时		节1 ①②③④ 节2 ①②③④
下半时		节3 ①②③④ 节4 ①②③④
决胜期		主教练挑战 □

证件号码	队员	号	上场队员	犯规 1 2 3 4 5

主教练 _____
第一助理教练 _____

B队

暂停		全队犯规
上半时		节1 ①②③④ 节2 ①②③④
下半时		节3 ①②③④ 节4 ①②③④
决胜期		主教练挑战 □

证件号码	队员	号	上场队员	犯规 1 2 3 4 5

主教练 _____
第一助理教练 _____

累积分

A	B	A	B	A	B	A	B
1	1	41	41	81	81	121	121
2	2	42	42	82	82	122	122
3	3	43	43	83	83	123	123
4	4	44	44	84	84	124	124
5	5	45	45	85	85	125	125
6	6	46	46	86	86	126	126
7	7	47	47	87	87	127	127
8	8	48	48	88	88	128	128
9	9	49	49	89	89	129	129
10	10	50	50	90	90	130	130
11	11	51	51	91	91	131	131
12	12	52	52	92	92	132	132
13	13	53	53	93	93	133	133
14	14	54	54	94	94	134	134
15	15	55	55	95	95	135	135
16	16	56	56	96	96	136	136
17	17	57	57	97	97	137	137
18	18	58	58	98	98	138	138
19	19	59	59	99	99	139	139
20	20	60	60	100	100	140	140
21	21	61	61	101	101	141	141
22	22	62	62	102	102	142	142
23	23	63	63	103	103	143	143
24	24	64	64	104	104	144	144
25	25	65	65	105	105	145	145
26	26	66	66	106	106	146	146
27	27	67	67	107	107	147	147
28	28	68	68	108	108	148	148
29	29	69	69	109	109	149	149
30	30	70	70	110	110	150	150
31	31	71	71	111	111	151	151
32	32	72	72	112	112	152	152
33	33	73	73	113	113	153	153
34	34	74	74	114	114	154	154
35	35	75	75	115	115	155	155
36	36	76	76	116	116	156	156
37	37	77	77	117	117	157	157
38	38	78	78	118	118	158	158
39	39	79	79	119	119	159	159
40	40	80	80	120	120	160	160

记录员 _____
助理记录员 _____
计时员 _____
进攻计时员 _____

得分		
节 ①	A _____	B _____
节 ②	A _____	B _____
节 ③	A _____	B _____
节 ④	A _____	B _____
决胜期	A _____	B _____

主裁判员 _____
副裁判员1 _____ 副裁判员2 _____
球队申诉队长签名 _____

最后比分　A 队 _____　B 队 _____
胜 队 _____
比赛结束时间（时：分）_____

图9　记录表

4.4 RECORDS – BEFORE THE GAME

4.4.1 SCORESHEET HEADER

Using the dark pen colour (black/blue), the scorer shall then enter in BLOCK CAPITALS:

- The names of the teams. First team "A" (the home team or in the case of tournaments or games on a neutral playing court, the first team named in the programme), and second team "B". If the names of the teams contain sponsors or nicknames, they should be included.

- The name of the competition.

- The game number.

- The date in the correct format (2 digits for the day, 2 digits for the month and 4 digits for the year, for example 02.05.2014).

- The official time that the game begins. Format: 24 hour digital clock, always using local time.

- The place (city and venue) of the game.

- The names of the Crew Chief and the Umpire(s). Format: last name in full, followed by the initial of the first name. For international competitions, the three-letter code (International Olympic Committee, IOC) for the referee's country shall be added after in brackets, for example BARTOW, K. (SWE).

4.4.2 RECORDING TEAMS: PLAYERS AND COACHES

The scorer shall then enter the names of the members of each team, using the list of team members as provided by the head coach or team's representative at least 40 minutes before the game is scheduled to begin.

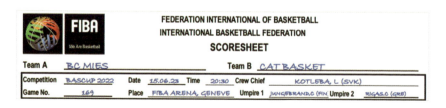

4.4 赛前应填写的内容

4.4.1 记录表的页眉

记录员应使用深色笔（黑色或蓝色）用印刷体大写字母填入以下信息：

- 球队名称。首先是"A"队（指主队，或是在赛会制或中立比赛场地中位于秩序册上靠前的球队），然后是"B"队。如果球队名称中包含赞助商或昵称，这些都应当被记录其中。
- 竞赛名称。
- 比赛序号。
- 正确格式的日期（2位数字表示日，2位数字表示月，4位数字表示年，例：02.05.2014）。
- 比赛正式开始的时间。格式：24小时制，总是使用当地时间。
- 地点（城市名称和比赛场馆）。
- 主裁判员和副裁判员的姓名。格式：填写完整的姓氏拼写，随后填写名字的首字母。对于国际比赛，应当在裁判员姓名后添加括号并填入代表其国籍的3位字母国家名称缩写〔参考国际奥委会（IOC）规定〕。例如：BARTOW, K.（SWE）。

4.4.2 填写球队信息：队员和教练员

随后，记录员应在记录表中填入球队人员名单。该名单应当由主教练或球队代表至少在预定的比赛开始前40分钟提交给记录员。

国际篮球联合会记录表

A队	BC MIES		B队	CAT BASKET	
竞赛名称：	BASCUP 2022	日期： 15.06.23	时间： 20:30	主裁判员：	KOTLEBA, L (SVK)
比赛序号：	169	地点： FIBA ARENA, GENEVE	副裁判员1： JUNGEBRAND,O (FIN)	副裁判员2：	RIGAS,C (GRE)

In the header, the scorer shall indicate the venue and the city where the game takes place.

Team 'A' shall occupy the upper part of the scoresheet, and team 'B' the lower part.

In the first column, the scorer shall enter the number (last three digits) of each player's license. For tournaments, the players' license numbers shall only be indicated for the first game played by the team.

In the second column, the scorer shall enter each player's name and initials, all in BLOCK CAPITAL letters. Each player's shirt number shall be

licence no.	Players		No.	Player in	Fouls				
					1	2	3	4	5
250	MAYER,	F.	0	⊗					
252	MANOS	J. Jr.	3	⊗					
253	JONES,	M.	4	X					
254	KENT,	Q.	5						
255	MARTINEZ,	C.	6						
256	LOPEZ,	J. (CAP)	7	⊗					
257	HEMEL,	D.	8						
265	OBRADOVIC,	C.	9						
266	AGUILAR,	V.	10						
268	RIMKUS,	T.	12						
300	PEROTTI,	R.	15	⊗					
301	VIDOT,	A.	20	⊗					
Head coach	0001 CANUT	J.							
First assistant coach	080 SERRAT	A.							

written in the third column. The captains of the teams shall be indicated by entering (CAP) immediately after their name.

At the bottom of each team's section, the scorer shall enter (in BLOCK CAPITAL letters) the names of the team's head coach and first assistant coach, and their license numbers. For tournaments, the coaches' license number shall only be indicated for the first game played by the team.

To make foul recording easier, the names of players shall be entered in increasing order of their shirt number (00, 0,1,2...99).

If a team presents fewer than twelve players, when the game starts, the scorer shall draw a line(s) through the last blank entry(ies). If there are more than one player blank entries, the horizontal line may reach the first box of players' fouls and continue diagonally to the last box (see example above). Such lines should not be ruled until after the head coach has signed.

4.4.3   STARTING FIVE AND HEAD COACHES' SIGNATURES

At least ten minutes before the game is scheduled to begin both head coaches shall confirm their agreement with the names and the corresponding numbers of their team members and the names of the head coach and first assistant coach.

Then the head coach shall indicate the five players to start the game by marking a small 'x' beside the players' number in the 'Player in' column, and will finally sign the scoresheet. The head coach of team

在页眉内，记录员应填写比赛场馆和城市名称。

"A"队应当占据记录表上半部分，"B"队占据下半部分。

在第一栏内，记录员应登记每名队员的证件号码（最后 3 位数字）。对于联赛，队员的证件号码只应在该队首场比赛时填写。

在第二栏内，记录员应登记

证件号码	队员		号	上场队员	犯规				
					1	2	3	4	5
250	MAYBR,	F.	0	Ⓧ					
252	MANOS	J. Jr.	3	Ⓧ					
253	JONES,	M	4	X					
254	KENT,	Q.	5						
255	MARTINEZ,	C.	6						
256	LOPEZ,	J. (CAP)	7	Ⓧ					
257	HEMEL,	D.	8						
265	OBRADOVIC,	C.	9						
266	AGUILAR,	V.	10						
268	RIMKUS,	T.	12						
300	PEROTTI,	R.	15	Ⓧ					
301	VIDOT,	A.	20	Ⓧ					
主教练	2001	CANUT	J.						
第一助理教练	C80	SERRAT	A.						

每名队员的姓和名字的首字母，都用印刷体大写字母。每名队员的上衣号码都应被登记在第三栏内。双方球队的队长在他们的姓名后面登记（CAP）。

在每队表格的底部，记录员应登记（用印刷体大写字母）该队主教练和第一助理教练的姓名和他们的证件号码。对于联赛，教练员的证件号码只应在该队首场比赛时填写。

为了更加方便地记录犯规，队员的姓名应按照其上衣号码的升序进行填写（00,0,1,2…99）。

如果一个球队出场少于 12 名队员，记录员应在比赛开始时在未使用的队员表格中画上贯穿空格的直线。如果有一个以上的队员空缺栏，那么所画的直线应从该队员犯规栏的第一个空格开始，直至该队员的空白栏的最后一个空格中止。只有主教练在记录表上签字确认名单以后，才可以画上这些直线。

4.4.3 首发队员和主教练的签字

至少在预定的比赛开始时间前 10 分钟，双方主教练应确认球队成员的姓名和相应的号码，以及主教练和第一助理教练的姓名。

随后主教练应指明比赛开始时上场的 5 名队员，并在队员号码旁边的"上场队员"栏内画一个小"x"（不套圆圈），最后主教练应在

'A' shall be the first to provide the above information.

At the beginning of the game, the scorer shall circle the small 'x' of the 5 players in each team to start the game (using the red pen). If there are any discrepancies the scorer must notify the referee immediately. During the game, the scorer shall draw a small 'x' (not circled) in the 'Player in' column when a substitute enters the game for the first time as a player.

Head coach	C001	CANUT A.			
First assistant coach	C120	BRAZAUSKAS, C.			

Players who have been designated by the head coach to start the game may be substituted in the event of an injury. In this case, the opponents are also entitled to substitute the same number of players, if they so wish.

If anyone (coaches, Table Officials, referees etc.) notice an error before the game, for example, that the number of a player recorded on the scoresheet is not the same as the number displayed on the shirt, or the name of a player is omitted on the scoresheet, the error must be immediately corrected. In particular, the wrong shirt number will be corrected or the name of the player will be added in the scoresheet without any sanction. If this kind of error is discovered when the game has already started, the Table Officials shall notify the referees, and the referee will stop the game at a convenient moment so as not to disadvantage either team. The wrong shirt number will be corrected without any sanction. However, the name of any player omitted from the scoresheet cannot be added to the scoresheet once the game has begun.

In the case of a team having no coach, the team's captain becomes responsible and shall sign the scoresheet in the box reserved for the head coach. In this case, the scorer shall also record the name of the captain in the head coach's box and then write after the word "CAP" (as shown).

Head coach	260	MARTINEZ, J. (CAP)			
First assistant coach					

4.4.4   PROCEDURE IN CASE OF GAME LOST BY FORFEIT

Game lost by forfeit

Remember, a team shall lose the game by forfeit if:

- The team is not present or is unable to field 5 players ready to play 15 minutes after the scheduled time to begin.

记录表上签字。"A"队主教练应首先提供上述资料。

在比赛开始时，记录员应在每一队比赛首发 5 名队员的小"x"上圈上圆圈（使用红笔）。如果上场队员与记录表信息存在任何差异，记录员应当立刻通知裁判员。比赛进行中，记录员应当在非首发队员首次替补进入比赛时在其"上场队员"栏内画一个小"x"（不套圆圈）。

| 主教练 | C001 | CANU̶T̶ A. | | |
| 第一助理教练 | C120 | BRAZAUSKAS, C. | | |

因为受伤，已经被主教练指定为比赛开始时上场的队员可以被替换。在这种情况下，如果对方也希望替换，他们有权替换相同数量的队员。

任何人（教练员、记录台人员、裁判员等）如果在赛前发现了场上错误，例如：队员登记号码与实际号码不符或队员姓名遗漏，这些错误必须立刻被纠正。尤其应当立刻纠正队员队服号码，添加遗漏队员姓名，无须进行额外的处罚。如果上述错误是在比赛开始后发现的，记录台人员应当通知裁判员，裁判员应当在不会置任何球队于不利的情况下停止比赛。在纠正错误的队服号码后，无须进行额外的处罚。但是，在比赛开始后，登记记录表时遗漏的队员姓名不能被添加到记录表上。

如果某队没有教练员，该队队长应在主教练栏中签字。在这种情况下，记录员应在主教练栏中登记该队队长的姓名并在他 / 她的姓名后登记"CAP"（如图显示）。

| 主教练 | 260 | MARTINEZ, J. (CAP) | | |
| 第一助理教练 | | | | |

4.4.4 比赛因弃权告负的程序

比赛因弃权告负

请牢记，如果球队：

- 在比赛预定的开始时间 15 分钟后不到场或不能使 5 名队员入场准备比赛。

- Its actions prevent the game from being played.

- It refuses to play after being instructed to do so by the referee.

If a team is not present at the venue, the scorer should complete the scoresheet in the usual way and in the boxes of the team players write "ABSENT" diagonally, over the players' names boxes. If both teams are not present, this procedure would be repeated in the boxes for each team. In any case, the pertinent explanations should be written on the back of the scoresheet.

Procedure:

- The scorer must register at least 5 players of the team that are present for the game.

- The head coach that is present, must give 5 starting players and sign the scoresheet.

- After waiting the prescribed time (15 minutes after the scheduled time to begin the game), and after being instructed by the referee, the scorer must disable the boxes where players register by writing: "ABSENT" as described above, for the team that is not present.

- The referees and Table Officials should also sign the scoresheet.

- The Crew Chief must write a brief report on the back of the scoresheet and must score 20-0 on the final score of the game, for the team present.

Team A

Licence no.	Players		No.	Player in	Fouls 1	2	3	4	5
250	MAYBR,	F.	0	X					
252	MANOS	J .Jr.	3	X					
253	JONBS,	M	4	X					
254	KBNT,	Q.	5						
255	MARTINBZ.,	C.	6						
256	LOPBZ,,	J. (CAP)	7	X					
257	HBMBL.,	D.	8						
265	OBRADOVIC,	C.	9						
266	AGUILAR,	V.	10						
268	RIMKUS,	T.	12						
300	PBROTTI,	R.	15	X					
301	VIDOT,	A.	20	X					
Head coach	2002	CANUT	J.						
First assistant coach	C20	SBRRAT	A.						

Team B

Licence no.	Players		No.	Player in	Fouls 1	2	3	4	5
		ABSENT							
Head coach									
First assistant coach									

Final Score	Team A	20	Team B	0
Name of winning team			BC MIES	

- 它的行为阻碍比赛继续进行。
- 在主裁判员通知比赛后拒绝比赛。

那么，该队由于弃权使比赛告负。

如果球队没有出现在比赛场地，记录员应如同正常情况般完成记录表，并且在球队队员姓名一栏斜着写上"弃权"。如果双方球队都没有出席，则应重复上述程序并在双方球队记录表的对应栏中进行登记。出现任何因弃权告负的情况，记录员都应在记录表背面写明相关理由。

程序：

- 记录员在赛前必须至少为到场的每支球队登记5名队员。
- 到场的主教练必须指定5名首发队员，并且在记录表上签字确认。
- 在比赛预定开始时间15分钟以后，经过裁判员的指示，记录员应当在记录表上队员姓名一栏中依照上述要求斜着填入"弃权"以示未到场的球队告负。
- 裁判员和记录台人员同样应在记录表上签字。
- 主裁判员必须在记录表的背面完成简短书面报告，确认20：0的最终比分和未到场的球队告负。

A队

证件号码	队员		号码	上场队员	犯规 1 2 3 4 5
250	MAYER,	F.	0	Ⓧ	
252	MANOS	J. Jr.	3	Ⓧ	
253	JONES,	M.	4	X	
254	KENT,	Q.	5		
255	MARTINEZ,	C.	6		
256	LOPEZ,	J. (CAP)	7	Ⓧ	
257	HEMEL,	D.	8		
265	OBRADOVIC,	C.	9		
266	AGUILAR,	V.	10		
268	RIMKUS,	T.	12		
300	PEROTTI,	R.	15	Ⓧ	
301	VIDOT,	A.	20	Ⓧ	
主教练	0001 CANUT	J.			
第一助理教练	C80 SERRAT	A.			

B队

证件号码	队员		号码	上场队员	犯规 1 2 3 4 5
	ABSENT				
主教练					
第一助理教练					

最后比分	A队 20	B队 0
胜队		BC MIES

4.5 THE RUNNING SCORE – DURING THE GAME

4.5.1   SCORES

The scorer shall keep a chronological running summary of points scored, by entering the field goals and the free throws made by each team.

There are four columns on the scoresheet for the running score. The two on the left are for team 'A' and the two on the right for team 'B'. The centre two columns are for the running score (160 points) for each team.

The scorer must use RED pen during the 1st and 3rd quarters, and DARK (blue or black) pen for the 2nd and 4th quarters and all overtimes (since overtimes are considered an extension of the 4th quarter).

When points are scored from field goals or free throws, the scorer shall record this as shown below.

One point: a filled circle (●) and beside it write the number of the player who scored the free throw.

In these examples, A8 and B14 each scored free throws.

	A	B	
6	50	50	4
8	51	51	14
	52	52	
	53	53	

Two points: a diagonal line (/) for right-handed and (\ ) for left-handed, and beside it write the number of the player who scored the field goal.

In this example, A10 scored a two-point field goal.

	A	B	
8	51	51	14
	52	52	
10	53	53	

	A	B	
8	51	51	14
	52	52	
10	53	53	

Three points: a diagonal line (/ or \ ) and by drawing a circle (O) around the player's number.

In this example, A8 scored a three-point field goal.

	A	B	
8	55	55	14
	56	56	
	57	57	
(8)	58	58	

4.5 累积分——赛中

4.5.1 得分

记录员应当按照时间顺序，以累积分的形式，记录球队的中篮和罚球得分。

记录表上，累积分一栏有 4 列空格。左侧两列记录"A"队得分，右侧两列记录"B"队得分。中间两列，为每支球队提供了最高 160 分的累积分序列。

记录员在第 1 节和第 3 节填写记录表时，必须使用红色笔，在第 2 节、第 4 节和所有决胜期，使用深色（蓝色或黑色）笔（因为所有决胜期都是第 4 节的延伸）。①

当队员在场上中篮或罚球得分，记录员应按照如下方式填写记录表。

1 分：在对应的实圆（●）旁登记罚球得分的队员号码。

在本例中，A8 和 B14 分别罚球得分。

	A	B	
6	50	50	4
8	51	51	14
	52	52	
	53	53	

2 分：在对应的斜线（右手画"/"，左手画"\"）旁登记中篮得分的队员号码。

在该举例中，A10 中篮得 2 分。

	A	B	
8	51	51	14
	52	52	
10	53	53	

	A	B	
8	51	51	14
	52	52	
10	53	53	

3 分：在对应的斜线（右手画"/"，左手画"\"）旁通过画一个圆圈（○）套住该队员的号码来记录。

在本例中，A8 中篮得 3 分。

	A	B	
8	55	55	14
	56	56	
	57	57	
⑧	58	58	

① 因为所有决胜期都是第 4 节的延伸，所以不更换用笔颜色。

- A field goal accidentally scored by a player in team's own basket shall be recorded as having been scored by the captain of the opposing team on the playing court.
- Points scored when the ball does not enter the basket (Art. 31 Goaltending and Interference) shall be recorded as having been scored by the player who attempted the field goal.
- At the beginning of each quarter the scorer shall continue to keep a chronological running summary of the points scored from the point of interruption (changing the pen's colour). All overtimes shall be written in the DARK colour (blue or black).

Closures: end of the quarter

At the end of each quarter, if there is no pending IRS situation, the scorer shall draw with the pen used in the quarter a thick circle (O) around the latest number of points scored by each team, followed by a thick horizontal line under those points and under the number of each player who scored those last points. If there is an IRS situation, the scorer cannot close the quarter until the referees make their final decision.

In addition, the scorer shall enter the score of that quarter in the proper section in the lower part of the scoresheet (using the colour of the quarter).

	A		B	
6	16	16	4	
8	17	17	14	
	18	18		
10	19	19	14	
	20	20	4	
8	21	21		
	22	22	14	
	23	23	10	
8	24	24		
	25	25		
6	26	26	6	

```
Scores  Quarter  ①   A   24      B   20
        Quarter  ②   A   ____    B   ____
        Quarter  ③   A   ____    B   ____
        Quarter  ④   A   ____    B   ____
        Overtimes     A   ____    B   ____
```

The scorer shall check the running score, foul counts and time-out counts with the visual scoreboard. If there is a discrepancy, and the score in scoreheet is correct, the scoreboard should be corrected immediately. If in doubt or if one of the teams raises an objection to the correction, the scorer shall inform the referee as soon as possible, but must wait for the first dead ball when the game clock is stopped before sounding the signal.

- 如果队员意外地使球进入本方球篮，应在记录表上登记在对方队的场上队长名下。
- 在球未中篮但判给得分的情况下（第31条 干涉得分和干扰球情况），得分应记录在试投队员名下。
- 每一节的开始，记录员应当按照时间顺序，从上一节比分的中断处继续记录（并更换用笔的颜色）。所有的决胜期，都应当使用深色（蓝色或黑色）笔填写。

一节的结束

在每一节比赛结束时，记录员应当用该节所使用的笔，在最后一次得分的分值上，画上一个空心圆圈（○）。随后，在该队最后得分和得分队员号码的单元格底端，画上一条水平线。如需要执行一次即时回放复审，记录员应在裁判员作出最终决定后才完结本节比赛。

除此之外，记录员还应当将本节比赛的得分填入记录表底端相应的球队本节得分栏（使用本节比赛所使用颜色的笔）。

	A		B
6	16	16	4
8	17	17	14
	18	18	
10	19	19	14
	20	20	4
8	21	21	
	22	22	14
	23	23	10
8	24	24	
	25	25	
6	26	26	6

得分　节 ① A _24_　B _20_
　　　 节 ② A ___　B ___
　　　 节 ③ A ___　B ___
　　　 节 ④ A ___　B ___
　　　 决胜期 A ___　B ___

记录员还应当检查累积分、犯规次数、暂停次数与可见的记录屏是否一致。如果不一致，并且记录表是正确的，记录屏应立即被纠正。如对此举产生疑问或有球队提出异议，记录员应尽快通知裁判员，但必须等到出现第一次死球，并且比赛计时钟停止时，才发出信号。

Overtime

In the case of overtimes the scorer shall draw, with the DARK pen, a thick circle (**O**) around the last number of points scored by each team, followed by a thick horizontal line under those points and under the number of each player who scored those last points.

In addition, the scorer shall enter the score of that quarter in the proper section in the lower part of the scoresheet.

	A		B	
	90	90		14
8	91	91		
	92	92		
	93	93		4
8	94	94		4
	95	95		

Scores	Quarter	①	A	_24_	B	_20_
	Quarter	②	A	_20_	B	_31_
	Quarter	③	A	_19_	B	_19_
	Quarter	④	A	_31_	B	_24_
	Overtimes		A	___	B	___

The end of game or the overtime

If at the end of the overtime the score is still tied, the scorer shall circle the final score of that overtime and draw a single thick horizontal line under those points and under the number of each player who scored those last points.

The partial score should not be recorded in the lower section of the scoresheet. This procedure shall be repeated for each overtime played until there is a winner.

Once the game is finished, the scorer shall circle the final scores of the last overtime and draw two thick horizontal lines under the final number of points scored by each team and the numbers of the players who scored those last points. A diagonal line shall also be drawn to the bottom of the column to obliterate the remaining numbers (running score) for each team. This is to be done in the DARK colour pen. The scorer shall then enter the TOTAL points scored in the overtimes in the lower section of the scoresheet.

At the end of the game, the scorer shall enter the final score and the name of the winning team.

	A		B	
	93	93		4
8	94	94		4
	95	95		
	96	96		
8	97	97		5
	98	98		
	99	99		
8	100	100		5
	101	101		
12	102	102		
	103	103		
	104	104		
	105	105		
	106	106		
	107	107		
	108	108		
	109	109		

Scores	Quarter	①	A	_24_	B	_20_
	Quarter	②	A	_20_	B	_31_
	Quarter	③	A	_19_	B	_19_
	Quarter	④	A	_31_	B	_24_
	Overtimes		A	_8_	B	_6_

决胜期

在每一决胜期结束时，记录员应当用深色笔，在最后一次得分的分值上，画上一个空心圆圈（〇），随后在该队最后的累积分分值和得分队员号码的单元格底端，画上一条水平线。

除此之外，记录员还应当将本节比赛的得分填入记录表底端相应的球队本节得分栏。

A		B	
	90	90	14
8	91	91	
	92	92	
	93	93	4
8	94	94	4
	95	95	

得分	节 ①	**A** _24_	**B** _20_
	节 ②	**A** _20_	**B** _31_
	节 ③	**A** _19_	**B** _19_
	节 ④	**A** _31_	**B** _24_
	决胜期	**A** ___	**B** ___

比赛或决胜期的结束

如果决胜期结束后比分依然相同，记录员应在最后的分值上画上圆圈。并且在最后的分值和最后得分队员的单元格下方画上单横线。

平局的决胜期得分不应被填写在记录表下方部分。该程序应重复至分出比赛胜负。

比赛结束时，记录员应在最后的决胜期结束时的分值上画上圆圈，并且在最后的分值和最后得分队员的单元格下方画上双横线。同时，在剩余的累积分表格中，画上斜线以使剩余表格失效。这些工作需要使用深色笔。随后，在记录表下方决胜期得分一栏中，记录员应分别填上每一队决胜期的总得分。

比赛结束后，记录员应填上比赛的最终得分和获胜球队。

A		B	
	93	93	4
8	94	94	4
	95	95	
	96	96	
8	97	97	5
	98	98	
	99	99	
8	100	100	5
	101	101	
12	102	102	
	103	103	
	104	104	
	105	105	
	106	106	
	107	107	
	108	108	
	109	109	

得分	节 ①	**A** _24_	**B** _20_
	节 ②	**A** _20_	**B** _31_
	节 ③	**A** _19_	**B** _19_
	节 ④	**A** _31_	**B** _24_
	决胜期	**A** _8_	**B** _6_

4.5.2 POSSIBLE MISTAKES AND SOLUTIONS

Mistakes can be corrected at any time before the Crew Chief signs the scoresheet at the end of the game, even if this correction influences the result of the game. The Crew Chief must sign next to the correction and report the error to the organisers of the game, by recording this on the back of the scoresheet.

Corrections on the scoresheet must be done clearly to preserve its readability and by using common sense according to the true sequence of the events.

If a mistake is discovered by the scorer:

- During the game, the scorer must wait for the first dead ball when the game clock is stopped, before sounding the signal and reporting the error to the referees. It is important to note that the Crew Chief is to be advised prior to any correction occurring. When the correction is complete the Crew Chief shall check it with a little signature with DARK pen as shown in the following examples.

- After the game, the Crew Chief will have to write a report at the back of the scoresheet, where all the mistakes have to be explained and validated.

The following mistakes could be made:

Case 1: Less points recorded

Three-point goal (scored by A8) recorded as two points.

The scorer shall draw a horizontal line to cancel the error and then record the correct score in the usual way.

A		B	
6	50	50	4
8	51	51	14
	52	52	
8	53	53	
(8)	54	54	
	55	55	

4.5.2 可能发生的错误和解决方案

记录表错误可以在比赛时间结束之后至主裁判员签字之前的任何时间被改正，即使这个改正会影响比赛的最终结果。主裁判员必须在错误改正处签字，并在记录表的背面作出说明，以向赛事组织者报告该情况。

记录表上的错误改正必须清晰、易读，并且按照比赛发展的顺序予以修正。

如果一个错误被记录员发现了：

- 在比赛中，记录员必须等到出现第一次死球，并且比赛计时钟停止时，才发出信号将错误报告给裁判员。最重要的是，要在任何的错误改正之前，通知主裁判员。完成错误改正后，主裁判员应在核实后在错误改正处使用深色笔签上名字。签字方法如下图所示。
- 在比赛结束后，主裁判员必须在记录表的背面以书面报告的形式写下所有错误的原因和修改理由。

可能发生下列错误：

案例 1：漏记了得分

3 分中篮（A8）被记录为 2 分。

记录员应当画上一条水平线，以取消错误的记录，然后在正确的位置如往常一样记录。

	A	B	
6	50	50	4
8	51	51	14
	52	52	
8	53	53	
8	54	54	
	55	55	

Case 2: More points recorded

Two-point goal (scored by A8) recorded as three points.

The scorer shall record immediately the correct score, but not draw a horizontal line to cancel the incorrect recording. Beside the incorrect score, a little dot (●) should be drawn to remember the error.

If a free throw is scored next by the team then this can be clearly indicated, as shown in the diagram.

	A	B	
6	50	50	4
8	51	51	14
	52	52	
8	53	53	
8	54	54	
	55	55	

Case 3: Recorded points for the incorrect team.

For the third case, we should follow the same procedure used for incorrectly awarded / recorded points.

The scorer shall record immediately the correct score, but not draw a horizontal line to cancel the incorrect recording. Beside the incorrect score, a little dot (●) should be drawn to remember the error.

The scorer must continue recording the points scored and use the blank spaces, if after the correction A8 scores a field goal followed by a free throw.

	A	B	
6	50	50	4
8	51	51	14
	52	52	
	53	53	
8	54	54	8
	55	55	

	A	B	
6	50	50	4
8	51	51	14
	52	52	
8	53	53	
8	54	54	8
	55	55	

案例 2：多记了得分

2 分中篮（A8）被记录为 3 分。

记录员应立即登记正确的得分，但不是画上一条水平线来取消错误的记录，而是应当在错误的累积分旁边画上一个实心圆点（●），来提示记住此处的错误。

如果下一次是罚球中篮得分，这个实心圆点可以提醒记录员正确地登记得分。

	A		B	
6	50	50	4
8	51	51	14
	52	52	
8	53	53	
8	54	54	
	55	55	

案例 3：将得分登记给了错误的球队

对于第 3 个案例，我们应当应用同样的程序来修改不正确的给予／登记得分。

记录员应立即登记正确的得分，但不是画上一条水平线来取消错误的记录，而是应当在错误的累积分旁边画上一个实心圆点（●），来提示记住此处的错误。

如果改正了错误后，A8 随后罚球中篮得 1 分，记录员必须在空白的空间连续登记比分．

	A		B	
6	50	50	4
8	51	51	14
	52	52	
	53	53	
8	54	54	8
	55	55	

	A		B	
6	50	50	4
8	51	51	14
	52	52	
8	53	53	
8	54	54	8
	55	55	

Case 3: ...continues

Only when the wrong score is passed (2 and 2 or 2 and 3 points), the scorer must draw a horizontal line across the incorrect fields.

In the example after the correction A9 scores a 2 points field goal twice.

Case 4: Wrong player's number for a made goal

If the scorer enters the wrong player's number after a made goal, the correct number should be written over the wrong one. Next to the corrected number, a little dot (●) should be drawn to remember the error.

Case 5: Wrong quarter score

This shall be simply corrected as shown in the diagram.

Case 6: Wrong type of foul

If the scorer enters a wrong type of foul, the correct type of foul should be written over the wrong one. Next to the foul, a little dot (●) should be drawn to remember the error.

Case 7: Foul entered to the wrong player

If the scorer enters a foul to the wrong player, the foul should be entered to the right player. Next to the wrong foul noted, a little dot (●) should be drawn to remember the error. Three different situations can occur:
- If this player commits the same type of foul later, the inscription will remain the same with the dot.
- if another type of foul is committed, the scorer will write it over the former one.
- if no other foul is committed, the scorer will strike a line on it.

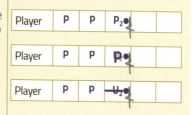

案例3：（续）

只有当被错误记录的分值超过（2分和2分，或2分和3分）时，记录员才应当在错误的得分区域内画上一条水平线。

在本案例中，经过改正之后，A9两次得2分。

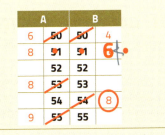

案例4：错误地登记了得分队员的号码

如果记录员在一次中篮后错误地登记了得分队员的号码，记录员应将正确的号码覆盖在错误的号码上。在修改后正确的号码旁应画上一个实心圆点（●），来提示记住此处的错误。

案例5：将得分登记到了错误的节次中

此类错误应按照图示方法进行改正。

案例6：登记了错误的犯规类型

如果记录员登记了错误的犯规类型，记录员应将正确的犯规类型覆盖在错误的犯规类型上。在修改后正确的号码旁应画上一个实心圆点（●），来提示记住此处的错误。

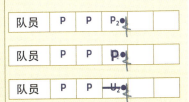

案例7：将犯规登记在了错误的队员名下

如果记录员将1次犯规登记在了错误的队员名下，记录员应将该犯规登记在正确的队员名下。在登记错误的犯规旁应画上一个实心圆点（●），来提示记住此处的错误。可能发生以下三种情况：

——如果该队员在随后的比赛中发生了同样类型的犯规，应保留原来填错的犯规内容。

——如果该队员在随后的比赛中发生了不同类型的犯规，记录员应在填错的内容上直接填写该不同类型的犯规。

——如果该队员在随后的比赛中没有发生犯规，记录员应在填错的内容上画上一条水平线。

If a mistake is discovered by the scorer:

- **At the end of the playing time** and before the scoresheet has been signed by the referee, the error should be corrected, even if this correction influences the result of the game. The referee must sign next to the correction and report the error to the organisers of the game, on the back of the scoresheet.

- **After the referee has signed the scoresheet,** no errors can be corrected. The referee or Commissioner, if present, must send a detailed report to the organising committee of the competition.

4.5.3   CLASSIFICATION OF THE FOULS

Player fouls may be personal, technical, unsportsmanlike or disqualifying and shall be recorded against the player.

Fouls committed by first assistant coach, substitutes, excluded players and accompanying delegation members may be technical or disqualifying and shall be recorded against the head coach. The scorer shall record fouls using the pen colour of the quarter.

Each time a new foul is recorded, the scorer must call out loud the personal foul reached by the player and team fouls (team fouled – and A-B team fouls), so the Table Officials crew is updated about records on the scoresheet (eg. 14B 4th personal – 3rd team foul – 2 – 3 team fouls), and with the help of colleagues (assistant scorer and/or timer) may check fouls recorded on the visible scoreboard.

All fouls shall be recorded, in the players and coach's boxes, as follows:

如果错误被记录员发现了：

- **在比赛时间结束之后**至主裁判员签字之前，该错误应被改正，即使这个改正会影响比赛的最终结果。主裁判员须签字确认这些修改，并通过在记录表的背面作出说明向竞赛的组织部门送交报告。

- **在主裁判员已在记录表上签字之后**，该错误不再可能被改正。主裁判员或到场的技术代表必须向竞赛的组织部门送交详细的报告。

4.5.3 犯规的分类

队员的犯规可能是侵人犯规、技术犯规、违反体育运动精神的犯规或取消比赛资格的犯规，这些犯规都应记录在队员名下。

第一助理教练、替补队员、出局的队员和随队人员的犯规可能是技术犯规或取消比赛资格的犯规，这些犯规应记录在主教练名下。记录员在记录犯规时，应当使用与该节填写记录表同色的笔。

每次记录犯规时，记录员都应大声说出这是该名队员和球队的第几次犯规（犯规队和双方全队犯规对比），以使记录台人员能够根据记录表更新记录屏的数据（**例如：B14，4次个人犯规；3次全队犯规；双方全队犯规2：3**）。同时，在同伴（助理记录员和/或计时员）的协助下，检查可见的记录屏上的犯规次数。

队员和教练员的犯规都应按下图所示被记录在对应的空格内：

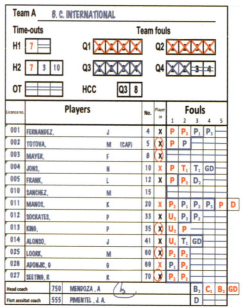

4.5.4   HOW TO RECORD THE DIFFERENT FOULS

Classification of the fouls

P	PERSONAL FOUL
T	TECHNICAL FOUL
U	UNSPORTSMANLIKE FOUL
D	DISQUALIFYING FOUL FOR PLAYER, HEAD COACH, FIRST ASSISTANT COACH, SUBSTITUTE, EXCLUDED PLAYER & ACCOMPANYING DELEGATION MEMBERS
F	DISQUALIFYING FOUL FOR FIGHTING ART. 39
C	TECHNICAL FOUL AGAINST THE HEAD COACH FOR PERSONAL BEHAVIOUR
B	TECHNICAL FOUL AGAINST THE HEAD COACH FOR BEHAVIOUR OF THE FIRST ASSISTANT COACH & ACCOMPANYING DELEGATION MEMBERS
GD	DISQUALIFICATION FOR PLAYER, HEAD COACH, FIRST ASSITANT COACH & ACCOMPANYING DELEGATION MEMBERS FOR COMBINATION OF TF´s OR UF´s

Note: If there is an IRS situation, the scorer shall wait for the referees' final decision before entering the corresponding fouls.

A队	B. C. INTERNATIONAL				
暂停			**全队犯规**		
上半时	7		节1 ⊠⊠⊠⊠	节2 ⊠⊠⊠⊠	
下半时	7	3	10	节3 ⊠⊠⊠⊠	节4 ⊠⊠ 3 4
决胜期				主教练挑战 Q3 8	

证件号码	队员			号码	上场队员	犯规 1 2 3 4 5
001	FERNANDEZ,	J		4	X	P P_2 P_1 P_3
002	TOTOVA,	M	(CAP)	5	Ⓧ	P P
003	MAYER,	F		8	Ⓧ	
004	JONS,	N		10	X	P T_1 T_1 GD
005	FRANK,	L		12	X	P P_2 D_2
010	SANCHEZ,	M		15		
011	MANOS,	K		20	X	P_3 P_1 P_2 P_3 P D
012	SOCRATES,	P		33	X	U_2 P_2
013	KING,	P		35	Ⓧ	U_2 P
014	ALONSO,	J		41	X	U_c T_1 GD
025	LOORK,	M		60	Ⓧ	P_3
026	ADONJIC,	G		69	X	P_1 P_3
027	SEETING, R	R		70	Ⓧ	P_2 P_3
主教练	750	MENDOZA , A				B_2 C_1 B_2 GD
第一助理教练	555	PIMENTEL , J.A.				D

4.5.4 如何登记不同的犯规

犯规的分类

P	侵人犯规
T	技术犯规
U	违反体育运动精神的犯规
D	队员、主教练、第一助理教练、替补队员、出局的队员和随队人员的取消比赛资格的犯规
F	因打架造成的取消比赛资格犯规（规则第 39 条）
C	因主教练自身原因导致的技术犯规
B	因助理教练和球队席成员所导致的主教练的技术犯规
GD	队员、主教练、第一助理教练、替补队员、出局的队员和随队人员因其技术犯规或违反体育运动精神的犯规的组合而被取消比赛资格

注意：如果出现了一次即时回放复审的情况，记录员应等到裁判员作出最终决定后才登记相应的犯规。

4.5.4.1   RECORDING AND DESCRIPTION OF THE PLAYERS FOULS

PERSONAL FOUL, WITHOUT FREE-THROWS

Player	P				

A personal foul shall be indicated by entering a 'P'.

PERSONAL FOUL, WITH 1, 2 or 3 FREE-THROWS

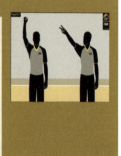

Player	P_1	P_2	P_3		

Any foul involving a free throw(s) shall be indicated by adding the corresponding number of free throws (1, 2 or 3) beside the 'P'.

FOULS WITH PENALTIES CANCELLED ACCORDING TO ART .42

Team A

Player	P	P_2	D_c		

Team B

Player	P	U_c			

All fouls against both teams involving penalties of the same severity and cancelled according to Art. 42 (Special situations) shall be indicated by adding a small 'c' beside the 'P', 'T', 'C', 'B', 'U' or 'D'.

4.5.4.1 登记和标注队员犯规

侵人犯规，罚则不包含罚球

队员	P				

一次侵人犯规应被登记一个"P"。

侵人犯规，罚则包含1次、2次或3次罚球

队员	P₁	P₂	P₃		

任何罚则包含罚球的侵人犯规都应在"P"旁登记罚球次数（1次、2次或3次）。

依据规则第42条而抵消罚则的犯规

A队

队员	P	P₂	D꜀		

B队

队员	P	U꜀			

对双方球队包含相同罚则并按规则第42条（特殊情况）被抵消的所有犯规，应在"P""T""C""B""U"或"D"的旁边登记一个小 "c"。

DOUBLE FOUL

Team A

Player	P			

Team B

Player	U_2	P		

A double foul is a situation in which 2 opponents commit personal, unsportsmanlike or disqualifying foul against each other at approximately the same time and both fouls have the same penalties.

TECHNICAL FOULS & COMBINATION

Player 1	T_1	T_1	GD		
Player 2	T_1	U_2	GD		
Player 3	T_1	P	P	P_2	T_1	GD

A technical foul against a player shall be indicated by entering a T followed by the corresponding number of free throw (1) beside T.

A second technical foul shall also be indicated by entering a 'T', followed by a 'GD' for the game disqualification in the following space.

A technical foul against a player with an earlier unsportsmanlike foul or an unsportsmanlike foul against a player with an earlier technical foul shall also be indicated by entering 'T' or 'U' followed by a 'GD' in the next following space.

双方犯规

A 队

队员	P			

B 队

队员	U₂	P		

双方犯规是两名互为对方的队员大约同时相互发生侵人犯规或违反体育运动精神的犯规或取消比赛资格的犯规的情况。

技术犯规和组合情况

队员 1	T₁	T₁	GD			
队员 2	T₁	U₂	GD			
队员 3	T₁	P	P	P₂	T₁	GD

队员的技术犯规应当被标记为 "T"。如果此犯规还带有罚球，则应在 "T" 旁标记罚球次数（1）。

第 2 次技术犯规同样需要填入 "T"，并在随后的空格内填入 "GD"，以表示该名队员已经被取消比赛资格。

一名队员在被宣判一起技术犯规之前，已经被宣判了一起违反体育运动精神的犯规；或是在被宣判一起违反体育运动精神的犯规之前，已经被宣判了一起技术犯规，则应在填入 "T" 或 "U" 后，在接下来的空格内填入 "GD"。

UNSPORTSMANLIKE FOUL & COMBINATION

Player 1	U₂	U₂	GD			
Player 2	T₁	U₂	GD			
Player 3	U₂	P	P	P₂	U₂	GD

An unsportsmanlike foul against a player shall be indicated by entering a 'U'. If it involves free throws they shall be indicated by adding the corresponding number of free throws (1, 2 or 3) beside the 'U'.

A second unsportsmanlike foul shall also be indicated by entering a 'U', followed by a 'GD' in the next following space.

An unsportsmanlike foul against a player with an earlier technical foul or a technical foul against a player with an earlier unsportsmanlike foul shall also be indicated by entering 'U' or 'T' followed by a 'GD' in the next following space.

DISQUALIFYING FOULS

Player	D₂				

A disqualifying foul shall be indicated by entering a 'D'. If it involves free throws they shall be indicated by adding the corresponding number of free throws (1, 2 or 3) beside the 'D'.

违反体育运动精神的犯规和组合情况

队员 1	U₂	U₂	GD			
队员 2	T₁	U₂	GD			
队员 3	U₂	P	P	P₂	U₂	GD

队员的违反体育运动精神的犯规应当被标记为"U"。如果此犯规还带有罚球，则应在"U"旁标记对应的罚球次数（1，2或3）。

第2次违反体育运动精神的犯规应同样填入"U"，并在随后的空格内填入"GD"，以表示该名队员已经被取消比赛资格。

一名队员在被宣判一起违反体育运动精神的犯规之前，已经被宣判了一起技术犯规；或是在被宣判一起技术犯规之前，已经被宣判了一起违反体育运动精神的犯规，则应在填入"T"或"U"后，在接下来的空格内填入"GD"。

取消比赛资格的犯规

队员	D₂				

取消比赛资格的犯规应当被标记为"D"。如果此犯规还带有罚球，则应在"D"旁标记罚球次数（1，2或3）。

4.5.4.2 RECORDING AND DESCRIPTION OF SUBSTITUTE & EXCLUDED PLAYER FOULS

TECHNICAL FOUL BY A SUBSTITUTE OR AN EXCLUDED PLAYER

Head coach	B_1			
Head coach	C_1	B_1	B_1	GD
Head coach	B_1	B_1	B_1	GD

A technical foul against a substitute or a excluded player for unsportsmanlike behaviour shall be indicated by entering 'B' in the head coach box, and adding the 1 free throw beside 'B'.

After a combination of the (3) technical fouls has been charged to the first assistant coach, substitute, excluded player or accompanying delegation members, a 'GD' shall be recorded against the head coach.

DISQUALIFYING FOUL BY A SUBSTITUTE

Substitute	D				
Head coach		B_2			

A disqualifying foul shall be indicated by entering a 'D' against the player. In addition, a bench technical foul for the head coach shall be entered. This foul does not count towards team fouls.

DISQUALIFYING FOUL BY AN EXCLUDED PLAYER

Excluded player	P	P	P_2	P_2	P	D
Head coach			B_2			

A disqualifying foul shall be indicated by entering a 'D' against the player. In addition, a bench technical foul for the head coach shall be entered. This foul does not count towards team fouls.

4.5.4.2 登记和标注替补队员和出局的队员的技术犯规

替补队员和出局的队员的技术犯规

主教练		B_1		
主教练		C_1	B_1	B_1	GD
主教练		B_1	B_1	B_1	GD

替补队员和出局的队员，因其违反体育运动精神的行为被宣判的技术犯规，应填入主教练犯规栏并登记为"B"，随后在"B"的旁边加上1次罚球。

当第一助理教练、替补队员、出局的队员或随队人员被宣判技术犯规累计达到3次时，主教练应被取消比赛资格，并在其犯规栏后登记"GD"。

替补队员的取消比赛资格的犯规

替补队员	D			
主教练		B_2		

替补队员的取消比赛资格的犯规应被登记为"D"。除此之外，登记主教练一次球队席人员的技术犯规。该犯规不计入全队犯规次数。

出局的队员的取消比赛资格的犯规

出局的队员	P	P	P_2	P_2	P	D
主教练			B_2			

出局队员的取消比赛资格的犯规应被登记为"D"。除此之外，登记主教练一次球队席人员的技术犯规。该犯规不计入全队犯规次数。

4.5.4.3 RECORDING AND DESCRIPTION OF HEAD COACH, FIRST ASSISTANT COACH & ACCOMPANYING DELEGATION MEMBERS FOULS

All fouls charged against the head coach do not count as team fouls. You will find below examples of disqualifying fouls because of fighting (Art. 39), with different penalties, whether the persons enter the court or actively participate in the fight etc.

TECHNICAL FOULS

Head coach	C_1		
Head coach	C_1	C_1	GD

A technical foul against the head coach for personal unsportsmanlike behaviour shall be indicated by entering a 'C'. A second similar technical foul shall also be indicated by entering a 'C', followed by a 'GD' in the following space.

Technical fouls during an interval of play are considered to be committed in the next quarter, using the pen colour of the quarter that follows, so it must be recorded as:

- B if the foul was committed by a first assistant coach, substitute, excluded player or an accompanying delegation member.
- C if the foul was committed by the head coach.

TECHNICAL FOUL BY FIRST ASSISTANT COACH, SUBSTITUTE, EXCLUDED PLAYER AND ACCOMPANYING DELEGATION MEMBER

Head coach	B_1			
Head coach	C_1	B_1	B_1	GD
Head coach	B_1	B_1	B_1	GD

A technical foul against a first assistant coach, substitute, excluded player and accompanying delegation member for unsportsmanlike behavior shall be indicated by entering a 'B' in the head coach box, and adding the 1 free throw beside 'B'.

After a combination of the (3) technical fouls has been charged to the first assistant coach or accompanying delegation members, a 'GD' shall be recorded against the head coach.

4.5.4.3 登记和标记主教练、第一助理教练和随队人员的犯规

所有登记在主教练名下的犯规均不计入全队犯规。下文中将对涉及打架情况（规则第 39 条）而被取消比赛资格的情况举例，这些情况有不同的罚则，无论是否有人员进入赛场积极参与了打架等。

技术犯规

主教练	C₁		
主教练	C₁	C₁	GD

对主教练由于自身违反体育运动精神的行为被宣判的技术犯规，应在记录表上登记为"C"。第二次由于类似原因被宣判的技术犯规，同样应被登记为"C"，并且在随后的空格内填入"GD"。

比赛休息期的技术犯规，应被认为是随后一节的犯规，应当使用下一节的记录笔来登记。因此，在记录时：

- 如果是由第一助理教练、替补队员、出局的队员和随队人员引起的犯规，登记为"B"。
- 如果是主教练犯规，登记为"C"。

第一助理教练、替补队员、出局的队员和随队人员的技术犯规

主教练	B₁			
主教练	C₁	B₁	B₁	GD
主教练	B₁	B₁	B₁	GD

因第一助理教练、替补队员、出局的队员和随队人员违反体育运动精神的行为被宣判的技术犯规，应填入主教练犯规栏并登记为"B"，随后在"B"的旁边加上 1 次罚球。

当第一助理教练或随队人员被宣判技术犯规累计达到 3 次时，主教练应被取消比赛资格，并在其犯规栏后登记"GD"。

DISQUALIFYING FOUL

Head coach	D_2		

A disqualifying foul against the head coach for personal unsportsmanlike behaviour shall be indicated by entering a 'D', adding the 2 free throws beside the 'D'.

DISQUALIFYING FOUL BY FIRST ASSISTANT COACH, SUBSTITUTE, EXCLUDED PLAYER OR ACCOMPANYING DELEGATION MEMBER

Head coach	B_2		
First assistant coach	D		

A disqualifying foul against a first assistant coach for personal unsportsmanlike behaviour shall be indicated by entering a 'D'. Also, a bench technical foul recorded as 'B' and adding the 2 free throws beside the 'B' should be entered in the head coach's box.

Head coach	B_2		

A disqualifying foul against an accompanying delegation member for personal unsportsmanlike behaviour shall be indicated by entering a 'B' and adding the 2 free throws beside the 'B' should be entered in the head coach's box.

取消比赛资格的犯规

主教练	D₂		

主教练由于自身违反体育运动精神的行为被宣判的取消比赛资格的犯规，应被登记为"D"，并在"D"的旁边加上2次罚球。

第一助理教练、替补队员、出局的队员和随队人员的取消比赛资格的犯规

主教练	B₂		
第一助理教练	D		

第一助理教练由于自身违反体育运动精神的行为被宣判取消比赛资格的犯规时，应当在其犯规栏内填入"D"。同时，应填入主教练犯规栏并登记为"B"，随后在"B"的旁边加上2次罚球。

主教练	B₂		

随队人员由于自身违反体育运动精神的行为被宣判取消比赛资格的犯规时，应当在主教练犯规栏内填入"B"，随后在"B"的旁边加上2次罚球。

4.5.4.4 RECORDING AND DESCRIPTION OF PLAYER & HEAD COACH FOULS

All fouls charged against the coach do not count as team fouls.

TECHICAL FOULS – UNSPORTSMALIKE FOULS & COMBINATION

Player	T_1	P	P	
Head coach			C_1	GD

Player-Head coach A1 has committed a technical foul during 1st quarter for faking a foul as a player. The technical foul shall be indicated against him/her as a player by entering a 'T_1'. In the 4th quarter he/she has been charged with a technical foul for personal unsportsmanlike behavior as a head coach, recorded as 'C_1', followed by 'GD' in the following space.

Player	U_2	P			
Head coach			B_1	B_1	GD

Player-Head coach A1 has committed an unsportsmanlike foul during 2nd quarter on B1 as a player. The unsportsmanlike foul shall be indicated by entering a 'U_2'. In the 3rd quarter he/she has been charged with a technical foul as a head coach for the physiotherapist's unsportsmanlike behaviour, recorded as 'B_1'. In the 4th quarter he/she has also been charged with a technical foul for an unsportsmanlike behaviour of substitute A6, recorded as 'B_1' against a head coach, followed by 'GD' in the following space.

Player	P	P	P	U_2	GD
Head coach			C_1		

Player-Head coach A1 has committed a technical foul during 2nd quarter for personal unsportsmanlike behavior as a head coach, recorded as 'C_1'. In the 4th quarter, he/she has committed an unsportsmanlike foul as a player, against B1. The unsportsmanlike foul shall be indicated by entering a 'U_2', followed by 'GD' in the following space.

4.5.4.4 登记和标注队员和主教练的犯规

所有登记在教练员名下的犯规不应记入全队犯规。

技术犯规、违反体育运动精神的犯规和组合情况

队员	T_1	P	P	
主教练			C_1	GD

队员兼主教练 A1 作为队员在第 1 节由于骗取犯规被宣判了一起技术犯规。该技术犯规应在他 / 她的犯规列表内被登记为"T_1"。在第 4 节，他 / 她作为主教练由于自身违反体育运动精神的行为被宣判了一起技术犯规，应被登记为"C_1"，在随后的空格内应登记"GD"。

队员	U_2	P		
主教练		B_1	B_1	GD

队员兼主教练 A1 作为队员，在第 2 节对 B1 发生一起违反体育运动精神的犯规，应被登记为"U_2"。他 / 她作为主教练，在第 3 节由于队医的违反体育运动精神的行为被宣判一起技术犯规，应被登记为"B_1"。在第 4 节，他 / 她又由于替补队员 A6 的违反体育运动精神的行为被宣判一起技术犯规，应被登记为"B_1"。在随后的空格内应登记"GD"。

队员	P	P	P	U_2	GD
主教练			C_1		

队员兼主教练 A1 作为主教练，在第 2 节由于自身违反体育运动精神的行为被宣判了一起技术犯规，应被登记为"C_1"。在第 4 节，他 / 她作为队员被宣判了一起对 B1 的违反体育运动精神的犯规，应被登记为"U_2"，在随后的空格内应登记"GD"。

4.5.4.5 RECORDING AND DESCRIPTION DISQUALIFYING FOUL ART.39 FIGHTS

**DISQUALIFYING FOUL FOR FIGHTING ART.39
BY A SUBSTITUTE OR AN EXCLUDED PLAYER**

Substitute 1	P	P	D	F	F	
Substitute 2	P	P	P_2	P_2	D	F
Head coach			B_2			
Excluded player	P	P	P_2	P_2	P	D_F
Head coach			B_2			

If the substitute has fewer than four fouls, then an 'F' shall be entered in all remaining foul spaces. If the player already has five fouls, then 'F' shall be written immediately after the fifth personal foul box (as shown above).

In addition, and regardless of the number of team members who leave the team bench area, only one technical foul shall be entered for the head coach recorded as B. Technical or disqualifying fouls according to Art. 39 shall not count as team fouls.

**DISQUALIFYING FOUL FOR FIGHTING ART.39 BY A SUBSTITUTE
OR AN EXCLUDED PLAYER ACTIVELY INVOLVED IN THE FIGHT**

Substitute 1	P	D_2	F	F	F	
Head coach		B_2				
Excluded player	P	P	P_2	P_2	P	D_2F
Head coach		B_2				

A disqualifying foul shall be indicated by entering a 'D', against the substitute or excluded player adding the 2 free throws beside 'D'.
If the substitute has fewer than four fouls, then an 'F' shall be entered in all remaining foul spaces.

If an excluded player is actively involved in a fight, then a 'D' shall be entered, adding the 2 free throws beside 'D'. Also, an 'F' shall be written immediately, below and next to the fifth personal foul box (as shown above).

In addition, a technical foul for the head coach 'B' shall be entered.

4.5.4.5 登记在打架情况中（规则第 39 条）发生的取消比赛资格的犯规

替补队员或出局的队员在一起打架中（规则第39条）被判取消比赛资格的犯规

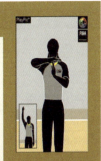

替补队员 1	P	P	D	F	F	
替补队员 2	P	P	P₂	P₂	D	F
主教练			B₂			

出局的队员	P	P	P₂	P₂	P	D_F
主教练			B₂			

如果一名替补队员的个人犯规次数少于 4 次，那么应在其剩余的犯规空格内填入"F"。如果一名队员已经个人犯规 5 次，那么应立刻在其空格后填入"F"（如上图所示）。

除此之外，不论由于离开球队席区域而被取消比赛资格的球队席人员的数量有多少，应登记主教练一次单一的技术犯规（"B"）。由于规则第 39 条而被宣判的技术犯规或取消比赛资格的犯规不应记入全队犯规。

替补队员或出局的队员在一起打架中（规则第39条）积极参与打架被判取消比赛资格的犯规

替补队员 1	P	D₂	F	F	F	
主教练		B₂				

出局的队员	P	P	P₂	P₂	P	D₂F
主教练			B₂			

应登记替补队员或出局的队员一起取消比赛资格的犯规"D"，随后在"D"的旁边加上 2 次罚球。如果该替补队员的个人犯规次数少于 4 次，那么应在其剩余的犯规空格内填入"F"。

如果一名出局的队员积极参与打架，应被登记一起取消比赛资格的犯规"D"，随后在"D"的旁边加上 2 次罚球。同时，应立刻在其第 5 次个人犯规后的下方填入"F"（如上图所示）。

除此之外，应登记主教练一次技术犯规"B"。

DISQUALIFYING FOUL FOR FIGHTING ART .39
BY A HEAD COACH, FIRST ASSISTANT COACH OR ACCOMPANYING
DELEGATION MEMBERS

If only the head coach is disqualified

Head coach	D_2	F	F

If only the first assistant coach is disqualified

Head coach	B_2		
First assistant coach	D	F	F

If both the head coach and the first assistant coach are disqualified

Head coach	D_2	F	F
First assistant coach	D	F	F

If an accompanying delegation member is disqualified

Head coach	B_2	(B)	

If two accompanying delegation members are disqualified

Head coach	B_2	(B)	(B)

Disqualifying fouls against head coaches, first assistant coaches and accompanying delegation members for leaving the team bench area (Art. 39), shall be recorded as shown above. In all remaining foul spaces of the disqualified person an 'F' shall be entered.

主教练、第一助理教练或随队人员在一起打架中
（规则第39条）被判取消比赛资格的犯规

如果只有主教练被取消比赛资格：

主教练	D_2	F	F

如果只有第一助理教练被取消比赛资格：

主教练	B_2		
第一助理教练	D	F	F

如果主教练和第一助理教练都被取消比赛资格：

主教练	D_2	F	F
第一助理教练	D	F	F

如果一名随队人员被取消比赛资格：

主教练	B_2	Ⓑ	

如果两名随队人员被取消比赛资格：

主教练	B_2	Ⓑ	Ⓑ

主教练、第一助理教练、替补队员和随队人员在打架情况中离开球队席区域（规则第39条），而被判取消比赛资格的犯规，登记方式应如上图所示。应在取消比赛资格的人员剩余的个人犯规空格内填入"F"。

DISQUALIFYING FOUL FOR FIGHTING (DF) ART .39
BY A HEAD COACH, FIRST ASSISTANT COACH OR ACCOMPANYING
DELEGATION MEMBERS ACTIVELY INVOLVED IN THE FIGHT

If only the head coach is disqualified

Head coach	D_2	F	F

If only the first assistant coach is disqualified

Head coach	B_2		
First assistant coach	D_2	F	F

A disqualifying foul shall be indicated by entering a 'D', and adding the 2 free throws beside the 'D', against the first assistant coach, then an 'F' shall be entered in all remaining foul spaces.

Also, a bench technical foul recorded as 'B' and adding the 2 free throws beside the 'B' should be entered in the head coach's box.

If both the head coach and the first assistant coach are disqualified

Head coach	D_2	F	F
First assistant coach	D_2	F	F

If an accompanying delegation member are disqualified

Head coach	B_2	B_2	

If two accompanying delegation members are disqualified

Head coach	B_2	B_2	B_2

A disqualifying foul for first assistant coach, shall be indicated by entering a 'D', and adding the 2 free throws beside the 'D', and the same each person disqualified, then an 'F' shall be entered in all remaining foul spaces.

Each disqualification of an accompanying delegation member shall be charged against the head coach, recorded as B_2, but shall not count to the three technical fouls for disqualification.

主教练、第一助理教练或随队人员在一起打架中（规则第39条）积极参与打架被判取消比赛资格犯规

如果只有主教练被取消比赛资格：

主教练	D_2	F	F

如果只有第一助理教练被取消比赛资格：

主教练	B_2		
第一助理教练	D_2	F	F

第一助理教练应被登记一起取消比赛资格的犯规"D"，并在"D"的旁边加上2次罚球，随后在其剩余的犯规空格内填入"F"。

同时，应填入主教练犯规栏并登记为"B"，随后在"B"的旁边加上2次罚球。

如果主教练和第一助理教练都被取消比赛资格：

主教练	D_2	F	F
第一助理教练	D_2	F	F

如果一名随队人员被取消比赛资格：

主教练	B_2	$⟨B_2⟩$	

如果两名随队人员被取消比赛资格：

主教练	B_2	$⟨B_2⟩$	$⟨B_2⟩$

第一助理教练取消比赛资格的犯规应被登记为"D"，并在"D"的旁边加上2次罚球，随后在其剩余的犯规空格内填入"F"，对其他每一名被取消比赛资格的成员同样应在其所剩余的个人犯规空格内填入"F"。

每一名随队人员取消比赛资格的犯规都应登记在主教练名下，记录为$⟨B_2⟩$，但不累计为主教练被取消比赛资格的3次技术犯规。

Is important to note that:

- During an interval of play, all team members entitled to play are considered as players (Art. 4.1.4).
- All team fouls committed in an interval of play shall be considered as being committed in the following quarter or overtime (Art. 41.1.2).
- All team fouls committed in an overtime shall be considered as being committed in the fourth quarter (Art. 41.1.3).

4.5.5 TEAM FOULS

For each quarter, four spaces are provided on the scoresheet (immediately below the team's name and above the players' names) to enter the team fouls.

Whenever a player commits a personal, technical, unsportsmanlike or disqualifying foul, the scorer shall record the foul against the team of that player by marking a large 'X' in the designated spaces in turn.

At the end of each quarter, unmarked spaces will be ruled out with two lines as shown below.

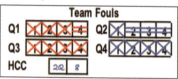

When a team reaches **its fourth team foul the team foul** marker shall be positioned on the scorer's table.

Where – at the end nearest to the bench of the team in a team foul penalty situation.

When – the ball becomes live following the fourth team foul in a quarter.

Who – The team marker may be lifted up by the table official nearest the bench of the team in a team foul penalty situation (e.g. assistant scorer, timer, shot clock operator).

以下几点非常重要：

- 在比赛休息期间，所有有资格参赛的球队成员，都被认为是队员（规则第 4.1.4 条）。
- 在比赛休息期间发生的所有全队犯规，应被认为是随后一节或决胜期比赛中的犯规（规则第 41.1.2 条）。
- 在决胜期内发生的所有全队犯规应被认为是发生在第 4 节内的犯规（规则第 41.1.3 条）。

4.5.5 全队犯规

记录表上为每支球队提供了每节 4 次的全队犯规记录表格（紧邻队名，并在队员名单之上）。

每当场上队员被宣判侵人犯规、技术犯规、违反体育运动精神的犯规或取消比赛资格的犯规时，记录员应当在全队犯规次数中进行记录，标记为"X"。

在每一节结束时，未被使用的全队犯规次数，应被记录员用两条平行线画掉，如下图所示。

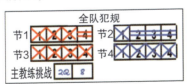

当一支球队在该节累计 **4 次全队犯规**后，记录员应将**全队犯规指示器**放置在记录台上。

位置——在记录台上最靠近球队席的一端。

时机——当某队在一节中全队犯规累计已达 4 次且球再次成为活球时。

操作员——记录台最靠近该球队席区域的人员（例如：助理记录员、计时员、进攻计时员）应立起全队犯规指示器。

Why – If the scorer lifts up the team marker and passes it to a colleague, this could distract the officials from the game that is about to restart. This could mean that there are fewer Table Officials watching the court and could result, for example, in the game clock being erroneously started later than it should be.

4.5.6   WHEN SUBSTITUTES ENTER THE GAME FOR THE FIRST TIME

During the game, the scorer shall draw a small 'x' (not circled) in the 'Player in' column, beside the number of a player when that player enters the game for the first time.

The scorer should use the pen colour of the quarter that is being played.

MANJOUR,	R. (CAP)	11	Ⓧ	P	42	P3	P2	
TOTEVA,	I.	12	X					
LEE,	A.	13	X	P2	P2			

4.5.7   TIME-OUTS

Each team may be granted:

- 2 time-outs during the first half,

- 3 time-outs during the second half with a maximum of 2 of these time-outs in the last 2 minutes of the second half,

- 1 time-out during each overtime.

Time-outs granted shall be recorded on the scoresheet by entering the minute of the playing time of the quarter or overtime in the appropriate boxes below the team's name. For example, if 3:44 minutes are left to the end of the first quarter, the scorer shall record 7, because 10-3 =7.

Unused time-outs may not be carried over to the next half or overtime. At the end of each half, (1st and 2nd quarter, 3rd and 4th quarter), unused time-outs will be ruled out with two horizontal lines as shown above.

Should the team not be granted its first time-out before the last 2 minutes of the second half, the scorer shall mark 2 horizontal lines in the first box for the team's second half.

原因——如果记录员将全队犯规指示器立起或转交给同事，这可能会使记录台人员对将要重新开始的比赛分心。这也可能意味着并不是每一个应当关注赛场的记录台人员都在关注赛场，从而可能导致例如计时钟被延时开动的情况。

4.5.6 替补队员第一次进入比赛

在比赛期间，当替补队员第一次作为队员进入比赛时，记录员应在队员号码旁边的"上场队员"栏内画一个小"x"（不套圆圈）。

记录员应使用本节比赛所使用颜色的笔。

MANJOUR.	R. (CAP)	11	Ⓧ	P	U2	P3	P2
TOTEVA,	I.	12	X				
LEE,	A.	13	X	P2	P2		

4.5.7 暂停

每支球队被准许：

- 上半时 2 次暂停。
- 下半时 3 次暂停，其中最后 2 分钟只允许请求 2 次暂停。
- 每一决胜期 1 次暂停。

被准予的暂停应被登记在记录表上，登记时须在球队名称下对应的空格内填入该节或决胜期此时的比赛时间（分钟）。例如：当第 1 节比赛剩余 3:44 时，记录员应当填入 7，因为 10−3=7。

未用过的暂停不得遗留给下半时或决胜期。在每半时结束时（第1、第 2 节结束和第 3、第 4 节结束时），未用过的空格用两条平行的横线标示（如上图所示）。

如果球队在第 4 节比赛计时钟显示 2:00 之前未登记其第一次暂停，记录员应在球队下半时暂停的第一个空格内画两条平行的横线。

4.5.8 HEAD COACH'S CHALLENGE

In games using the Instant Replay System (IRS), a Head Coach's Challenge (HCC) is available to each team and may be requested at any time during the game.

The head coach requesting the challenge shall make eye contact with the nearest referee and clearly say loudly in English "challenge" while showing the head coach challenge signal (No. 58, drawing a box, like a TV screen). The request shall be final and irreversible.

If granted, the HCC shall be recorded on the scoresheet, below the team name, in the boxes next to HCC. In the first box, the scorer shall enter the quarter or overtime (Q1, Q2, Q3, Q4 or OT) and in the second box the minute of playing time of the quarter or overtime.

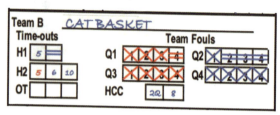

4.5.9 END OF QUARTER OR INTERVAL PLAY

- Recording the partial scores, fouls and unused time-outs.
- With two horizontal parallel lines (as described above):
  - At the end of each quarter unmarked team foul spaces.
  - At the end of each half unused time-outs (above).

At the end of 2nd quarter (first half), the scorer shall draw a thick line between the spaces that have been used and those that have not been used in the players' personal foul boxes and the coach's foul boxes. These lines shall be drawn in the DARK colour (blue or /black).

4.5.8 主教练挑战

在所有使用即时回放系统（IRS）的比赛中，主教练可以请求一次主教练挑战（HCC），并可以在比赛中的任何时间请求该挑战。

主教练应与最靠近的裁判员建立目光联系并清楚地提出主教练挑战，并应用英语大声说出"challenge"（挑战），同时做出主教练挑战手势（58号手势，用手画出一个长方形，就像电视屏幕）。该请求应是最终且不可取消的。

被准予的主教练挑战应登记在球队名称下"主教练挑战"（HCC）旁的空格内。记录员应在第一个空格内填入某节或决胜期（Q1、Q2、Q3、Q4或OT），并在第二个空格内填入该节或决胜期此时的比赛时间（分钟）。

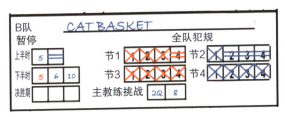

4.5.9 一节或比赛休息期间的结束

- 记录此时的比分、犯规和未用过的暂停。
- 下列情况中，未用过的空格用两条平行的横线标示：
  - 每节结束时，未标示的全队犯规空格。
  - 每半时结束时，未用过的暂停。

在第2节（上半时）结束时，记录员应在队员个人犯规栏和教练员的犯规栏中在已经被用过的和那些还未被用过的方格之间画一条粗线。这些线应当使用深色（蓝色或黑色）笔。

The scoresheet should be made available to the Commissioner and Referee whenever they request to see it.

MAYER,	F.	0	Ⓧ	P3	P	P		
MANOS	J Jr.	3	Ⓧ	P	P			
JONES,	M	4	X					
KENT,	Q.	5	X					

4.5.10   *PROCEDURE IN CASE OF GAME LOST BY DEFAULT*

Game lost by default

A team shall lose a game by default if, during the game, the team has fewer than two players on the playing court ready to play.

- If the team to which the game is awarded is ahead, the final score shall stand as at the time when the game was stopped. If the team to which the game is awarded is not ahead, the score shall be recorded as 2 to 0 in its favour.

- The referees and Table Officials should also sign the scoresheet. The referee should also make a record on the back of the scoresheet for the organising body.

- The referee must write the report for the organization on the back of the scoresheet, and will also write either current result of the game or 2-0, depending on who has run out of players to play.

无论何时，只要技术代表和裁判员提出查看记录表的要求，记录员应当即刻将记录表递交给他们。

MAYER,	F.	0	Ⓧ	P₃	P	P		
MANOS	J Jr.	3	Ⓧ	P	P			
JONES,	M	4	X					
KENT,	Q.	5	X					

4.5.10 比赛因缺少队员告负的程序

比赛因缺少队员告负

在比赛中，如果某队在比赛场地上准备比赛的队员少于2名，该队将因缺少队员使比赛告负。

- 如判获胜的队领先，则在比赛停止时的比分应有效。如判获胜的队不领先，则比分应记录为 2：0，对该队有利。
- 裁判员和记录台人员仍然应在记录表上签字。主裁判员还应在记录表背面作书面报告提供给竞赛的组织部门。
- 主裁判员必须在记录表背面作书面报告提供给竞赛的组织部门。同时，还应写明结束时的比分或 2：0 的比分，以说明是因为哪支球队的原因致使比赛结束。

4.6 AT THE END OF THE GAME

4.6.1 RECORDING THE FINAL SCORE

At the end of the game (4th quarter or the last overtime), the scorer shall draw 2 thick horizontal lines under the final number of points scored by each team and the numbers of the players who scored those last points as shown.

A diagonal line should also be drawn to the bottom of the column from left to right to cancel the remaining numbers (running score) for each team as shown.

The partial score of that quarter has to be recorded, as well as the final score and the name of the winning team (including any sponsors name).

The official time when the game ended has to be recorded. Format: 24-hour digital clock, always using local time.

	A	B	
8	86	86	4
8	87	87	14
	88	88	14
10	89	89	
	90	90	14
8	91	91	
	92	92	
	93	93	(4)
(8)	(94)	(94)	4
	95	95	
	96	96	
(8)	97	97	(5)
	98	98	
	99	99	
(8)	(100)	(100)	(5)
	101	101	
12	(102)	102	
	103	103	
	104	104	
	105	105	
	106	106	
	107	107	
	108	108	
	109	109	

Scores	Quarter ①	A _25_	B _17_
	Quarter ②	A _16_	B _27_
	Quarter ③	A _24_	B _30_
	Quarter ④	A _25_	B _16_
	Overtimes	A _13_	B _7_

Final Score	Team A _103_ Team B _97_
Name of winning team	CLUB YMKA
Game ended at (hh:mm)	22:25

4.6 比赛结束时

4.6.1 记录最终比分

全场比赛结束时（第 4 节或最后的决胜期），记录员应当在球队累积分分值和最后得分队员表格的最下方，画上两条粗水平线。

随后，记录员需要在剩余的累积分和得分队员空格内，为每支球队单独画上一条斜线（如图所示）。

同时，记录员还要记录每一节的球队得分、比赛最终得分和胜队名称（包括赞助商的名字）。

最后，记录员要记录比赛结束的官方时间。格式：24 小时制，一贯使用当地时间。

得分	节 ①	A	**25**	B	**17**
	节 ②	A	16	B	**27**
	节 ③	A	**24**	B	30
	节 ④	A	25	B	16
	决胜期	A	13	B	7

最后比分	A队	103	B队	97
胜队		CLUB YMKA		
比赛结束时间（时：分）		22:25		

	A	B	
8	86	86	4
8	87	87	14
	88	88	14
10	89	89	
	90	90	14
8	91	91	
	92	92	
	93	93	④
⑧	⑨4	⑨4	4
	95	95	
	96	96	
⑧	97	97	⑤
	98	98	
	99	99	
⑧	⑩⑩	⑩⑩	⑤
12	⑩②2	102	
	103	103	
	104	104	
	105	105	
	106	106	
	107	107	
	108	108	
	109	109	

4.6.2 FINISH THE FOOTER AND SIGNATURE OF THE CREW

At the end of the game, the scorer will review the scoresheet and draw a line through each team's unused boxes as shown. There is no difference made between players who did not show up and those who were on the bench but did not enter the court.

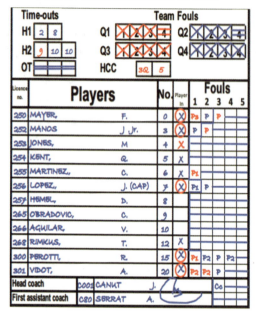

The scorer shall then enter his/her surname on the scoresheet in block capital letters and then sign. After this, the assistant scorer, timer and the 24 second operator, shall enter their details, as shown. The scorer shall draw a horizontal line through each of the 'Captain's signature in case of protest' boxes.

Once signed by the Umpire(s), the Crew Chief shall be the last to approve and sign the scoresheet.

The Crew Chief's signature, terminates the officials' administration and connection with the game, except if one of the captains signs the scoresheet under protest (using the space marked 'Captain's signature in case of protest'). If this occurs, the Table Officials and the Umpire(s) shall remain at the disposal of the referee and the Commissioner (if present) until the Crew Chief gives them permission to leave.

Scorer	ISOLA,	D.	
Assistant scorer	WAVE,	M.	
Timer	FERNANDEZ,	P.	
Shot clock operator	PATTON,	M.	

4.6.2 填写页脚和执裁团队签字

比赛结束后，记录员应当重新检查记录表，并且在每支球队未被使用的空白表格中画上单横线（如图所示）。在名单上被填写的队员，不管是未来到现场还是未上场比赛，记录员都应在其空白表格中画上单横线。

记录员应在记录表上用大写字母填入他／她的姓氏并签字。随后，助理记录员、计时员和进攻计时员，也应当填入他们的信息并签字，如图所示。记录员应在"球队申诉队长签名"一栏画上单横线。

在副裁判员（们）在记录表上签字后，主裁判员应最后批准并在记录表上签字。

主裁判员的签字结束了裁判员对比赛的管理和联系，如果某队长在记录表申诉格内（标示"球队申诉队长签名"的栏内）签字，记录台人员和副裁判员（们）应在主裁判员和到场的技术代表进行处理的过程中留下，直到他／她允许大家离开。

记录员	ISOLA,	D.	
助理记录员	WAVE,	M.	
计时员	FERNANDEZ,	P.	
进攻计时员	PATTON,	M.	

4.7 SUMMARY OF PEN COLOURS

Two colours will be used to fill the scoresheet: DARK blue / black and red.

Blue or Black Colour

Scoresheet Header

- Team's full names.
- Competition.
- Date (day.month.year: dd.mm.yyyy, for example 24.08.2007).
- Game starting time.
- Game number.
- Place of the game.
- Referee's surnames, initials of their names and their home countries.

Teams

- Team's names.
- Players and coaches' surnames and initials of their names.
- Players' shirt numbers.
- Last three digits of the players and coaches' license numbers.
- The cross ("X") corresponding to the starting five players from each team.
- The coaches' signatures confirming their agreement with the names and corresponding numbers of their team members and the coaches' names.
- The line drawn through the spaces for the license number, name, number, etc. when a team presents fewer than twelve players (line drawn after the game has begun).
- Fouls committed by players in the 2nd and 4th quarter (and overtimes).
- Time-outs and Head Coach's Challenges of the 2nd and 4th quarter (and overtimes).
- Team fouls of the 2nd and 4th quarter (and overtimes).
- Players who enter the court to play for the first time in the 2nd and 4th quarter (and overtimes).

4.7 用笔的颜色

记录表应当使用两种颜色的笔来填写：深色笔（蓝色笔或黑色笔）和红色笔。

蓝色笔或黑色笔

记录表表头

- 球队全称。
- 比赛信息。
- 日期（日 . 月 . 年，例如：24.08.2007 ）。
- 比赛开始时间。
- 比赛场序。
- 比赛地点。
- 裁判员姓氏、名字首字母、国籍。

球队

- 双方队名。
- 队员和教练员的姓氏，以及他们名字的首字母。
- 队员上衣的号码。
- 队员和教练员证件号码的后 3 位。
- 在每队首发队员对应的空格中标记 "X"。
- 双方主教练签字确认本队队员姓名与号码是否一致，确认教练员的姓名。
- 当球队报名少于 12 名队员时，在证件号码、姓名、号码等队员个人信息表格中画上水平线（在比赛开始后画）。
- 记录队员第 2 节、第 4 节（和所有决胜期）个人犯规的情况。
- 记录球队第 2 节、第 4 节（和所有决胜期）暂停和主教练挑战的情况。
- 记录球队第 2 节、第 4 节（和所有决胜期）全队犯规的情况。
- 记录球队第 2 节、第 4 节（和所有决胜期）队员首次上场比赛的情况。

- The thick line drawn at the end of the 2nd quarter between the foul spaces that have been used and those that have not been used.
- The thick diagonal line drawn at the end of the playing time obliterating the remaining spaces.

Scoresheet footer

- The score of 2nd quarter and 4th quarter.
- The final score of the game.
- The name of the winning team.
- The captain's signature in case of protest or the thick line drawn if it was not used.
- Table Officials' surnames, initials of their names and their license numbers.
- The signatures of the officiating crew members (referees and Table Officials) .

Running score

- The running score during the 2nd and 4th quarter.
- The running score of the overtime(s).

Red Colour

Teams

- Time-outs and Head Coach's Challenges of the 1st and 3rd quarter.
- Fouls committed by players in the 1st and 3rd quarter.
- Team fouls of the 1st and 3rd quarter.
- Players who enter the court to play for the first time in the 1st and 3rd quarter.
- The circle around the cross of the starting five players of both teams as they enter the court to start the game.

Running score

- The running score of the 1st and 3rd quarter .

Scoresheet footer

- The score of 1st quarter and 3rd quarter.

- 第 2 节结束后，使用粗线分隔已经使用和未被使用的队员个人犯规表格。
- 比赛结束后，使用粗斜线分隔已被使用和未被使用的表格。

记录表页脚

- 记录第 2 节和第 4 节的得分。
- 记录比赛最终比分。
- 记录获胜队的队名。
- 队长在记录表申诉格内签字，或在未申诉的情况下画上一条粗线。
- 填写记录台人员的姓氏、名字首字母和证件号码。
- 执裁团队（裁判员和记录台人员）在记录表上签字。

累积分

- 记录第 2 节和第 4 节的累积分。
- 记录每一个决胜期的累积分。

红笔

球队

- 记录球队第 1 节、第 3 节暂停和主教练挑战的情况。
- 记录队员第 1 节、第 3 节个人犯规的情况。
- 记录球队第 1 节、第 3 节全队犯规的情况。
- 记录球队第 1 节、第 3 节队员首次上场比赛的情况。
- 在每一队比赛首发队员进入赛场准备开始比赛时在"X"上画一个圆圈。

累积分

- 记录第 1 节和第 3 节的累积分。

记录表页脚

- 记录第 1 节和第 3 节的得分。

4.8 EXAMPLES OF SCORESHEETS

4.8.1 BEFORE THE GAME

FEDERATION INTERNATIONAL OF BASKETBALL
INTERNATIONAL BASKETBALL FEDERATION

SCORESHEET

Team A **BC MIES**   Team B **CAT BASKET**

| Competition | BASCUP 2022 | Date | 15.06.23 | Time | 20:30 | Crew Chief | KOTLEBA, L (SVK) |
| Game No. | 169 | Place | FIBA ARENA, GENEVE | Umpire 1 | JUNGEBRAND,O (FIN | Umpire 2 | RIGAS,O (GRE) |

Team A BC MIES

Time-outs

H1		Q1	1 2 3 4	Q2	1 2 3 4
H2		Q3	1 2 3 4	Q4	1 2 3 4
OT		HCC	

Team Fouls

Licence no.	Players		No.	Player In	Fouls 1 2 3 4 5
250	MAYER,	F.	0		
252	MANOS	J. Jr.	3		
253	JONES,	M.	4		
254	KENT,	Q.	5		
255	MARTINEZ,	O.	6		
256	LOPEZ,	J. (CAP)	7		
257	HEMEL,	D.	8		
265	OBRADOVIC,	O.	9		
266	AGUILAR,	V.	10		
268	RIMKUS,	T.	12		
300	PEROTTI,	R.	15		
301	VIDOT,	A.	20		

| Head coach | C001 | CANUT | J. |
| First assistant coach | C80 | SERRAT | A. |

Team B CAT BASKET

Time-outs

H1		Q1	1 2 3 4	Q2	1 2 3 4
H2		Q3	1 2 3 4	Q4	1 2 3 4
OT		HCC	

Team Fouls

Licence no.	Players		No.	Player In	Fouls 1 2 3 4 5
500	RADONJIC,	G.	4		
501	MANTILA,	P.	5		
502	TANABE,	V.	6		
503	PUIG,	J.	7		
505	THRON,	H.	8		
506	MITLECH,	J.	9		
700	MARTI,	O.	10		
750	MANJOUR,	R. (CAP)	11		
751	TOTEVA,	L.	12		
766	LEE,	A.	13		
800	KEM,	B.	14		

| Head coach | C50 | CASTRO | A. |
| First assistant coach | C111 | AURISNMA | J.M. |

Scorer	ISOLA,	D.
Assistant scorer	ONNA,	M.
Timer	FERNANDEZ,	P.
Shot clock operator	PATTON,	M.

RUNNING SCORE

A	B	A	B	A	B	A	B
1 1		41 41		81 81		121 121	
2 2		42 42		82 82		122 122	
3 3		43 43		83 83		123 123	
4 4		44 44		84 84		124 124	
5 5		45 45		85 85		125 125	
6 6		46 46		86 86		126 126	
7 7		47 47		87 87		127 127	
8 8		48 48		88 88		128 128	
9 9		49 49		89 89		129 129	
10 10		50 50		90 90		130 130	
11 11		51 51		91 91		131 131	
12 12		52 52		92 92		132 132	
13 13		53 53		93 93		133 133	
14 14		54 54		94 94		134 134	
15 15		55 55		95 95		135 135	
16 16		56 56		96 96		136 136	
17 17		57 57		97 97		137 137	
18 18		58 58		98 98		138 138	
19 19		59 59		99 99		139 139	
20 20		60 60		100 100		140 140	
21 21		61 61		101 101		141 141	
22 22		62 62		102 102		142 142	
23 23		63 63		103 103		143 143	
24 24		64 64		104 104		144 144	
25 25		65 65		105 105		145 145	
26 26		66 66		106 106		146 146	
27 27		67 67		107 107		147 147	
28 28		68 68		108 108		148 148	
29 29		69 69		109 109		149 149	
30 30		70 70		110 110		150 150	
31 31		71 71		111 111		151 151	
32 32		72 72		112 112		152 152	
33 33		73 73		113 113		153 153	
34 34		74 74		114 114		154 154	
35 35		75 75		115 115		155 155	
36 36		76 76		116 116		156 156	
37 37		77 77		117 117		157 157	
38 38		78 78		118 118		158 158	
39 39		79 79		119 119		159 159	
40 40		80 80		120 120		160 160	

Scores	Quarter ①	A ___	B ___
	Quarter ②	A ___	B ___
	Quarter ③	A ___	B ___
	Quarter ④	A ___	B ___
	Overtimes	A ___	B ___

Crew Chief	_____	Final Score	Team A ___	Team B ___
Umpire 1	_____ Umpire 2 _____	Name of winning team	_____
Captain'signature in case of protest	_____	Game ended at (hh:mm)	_____

4.8 记录表范例

4.8.1 比赛开始前

国际篮球联合会记录表

A队 _BC MIES_   B队 _CAT BASKET_

竞赛名称	BASCUP 2022	日期 15.06.23 时间 20:30	主裁判员 KOTLEBA, L (SVK)
比赛序号	169	地点 FIBA ARENA, GENEVE	副裁判员1 JUNGEBRAND,C (FIN) 副裁判员2 RIGAS,C (GRE)

A 队   BC MIES

暂停   全队犯规
上半时   节1 1 2 3 4   节2 1 2 3 4
下半时   节3 1 2 3 4   节4 1 2 3 4
决胜期   主教练挑战

累积分

证件号码	队 员	号	上场队员	犯 规 1 2 3 4 5
250	MAYER, F.	0		
252	MANOS, J. Jr.	3		
253	JONES, M	4		
254	KENT, Q.	5		
255	MARTINEZ, C.	6		
256	LOPEZ, J. (CAP)	7		
257	HEMEL, D.	8		
265	OBRADOVIC, C.	9		
266	AGUILAR, V.	10		
268	RIMKUS, T.	12		
300	PEROTTI, R.	15		
301	VIDOT, A.	20		

主教练   C001 CANUT J.
第一助理教练   C80 SERRAT A.

B队   CAT BASKET

暂停   全队犯规
上半时   节1 1 2 3 4   节2 1 2 3 4
下半时   节3 1 2 3 4   节4 1 2 3 4
决胜期   主教练挑战

证件号码	队 员	号	上场队员	犯 规 1 2 3 4 5
500	RADONJIC, G.	4		
501	MANTILA, P.	5		
502	TANABE, V.	6		
503	PUIG, J.	7		
505	THRON, H.	8		
506	MITLSCH, J.	9		
700	MARTI, C.	10		
750	MANJOUR, R. (CAP)	11		
751	TOTEVA, I.	12		
766	LEE, A.	13		
800	KEM, B.	14		

主教练   C50 CASTRO A.
第一助理教练   C111 AURIENMA J.M.

累积分表:

A	B	A	B	A	B	A	B	A	B
1	1	41	41	81	81	121	121		
2	2	42	42	82	82	122	122		
3	3	43	43	83	83	123	123		
4	4	44	44	84	84	124	124		
5	5	45	45	85	85	125	125		
6	6	46	46	86	86	126	126		
7	7	47	47	87	87	127	127		
8	8	48	48	88	88	128	128		
9	9	49	49	89	89	129	129		
10	10	50	50	90	90	130	130		
11	11	51	51	91	91	131	131		
12	12	52	52	92	92	132	132		
13	13	53	53	93	93	133	133		
14	14	54	54	94	94	134	134		
15	15	55	55	95	95	135	135		
16	16	56	56	96	96	136	136		
17	17	57	57	97	97	137	137		
18	18	58	58	98	98	138	138		
19	19	59	59	99	99	139	139		
20	20	60	60	100	100	140	140		
21	21	61	61	101	101	141	141		
22	22	62	62	102	102	142	142		
23	23	63	63	103	103	143	143		
24	24	64	64	104	104	144	144		
25	25	65	65	105	105	145	145		
26	26	66	66	106	106	146	146		
27	27	67	67	107	107	147	147		
28	28	68	68	108	108	148	148		
29	29	69	69	109	109	149	149		
30	30	70	70	110	110	150	150		
31	31	71	71	111	111	151	151		
32	32	72	72	112	112	152	152		
33	33	73	73	113	113	153	153		
34	34	74	74	114	114	154	154		
35	35	75	75	115	115	155	155		
36	36	76	76	116	116	156	156		
37	37	77	77	117	117	157	157		
38	38	78	78	118	118	158	158		
39	39	79	79	119	119	159	159		
40	40	80	80	120	120	160	160		

记录员   ISOLA, D.
助理记录员   ONNA, M.
计时员   FERNANDEZ, P.
进攻计时员   PATTON, M

得分 节① A   B
     节② A   B
     节③ A   B
     节④ A   B
     决胜期 A   B

主裁判员 _____

副裁判员1 _____   副裁判员2 _____

球队申诉队长签名 _____

最后比分   A队 _____   B队 _____
胜 队 _____
比赛结束时间（时：分）_____

4.8.2 END OF 1ST QUARTER

FIBA
We Are Basketball

FEDERATION INTERNATIONAL OF BASKETBALL
INTERNATIONAL BASKETBALL FEDERATION

SCORESHEET

Team A: **BC MIES**   Team B: **CAT BASKET**

Competition	BASCUP 2022	Date 15.06.23	Time 20:30	Crew Chief	KOTLEBA, L. (SVK)
Game No.	169	Place FIBA ARENA, GENEVE	Umpire 1 JUNGEBRAND,C (FIN)	Umpire 2	RIGAS,C (GRE)

Team A BC MIES

Time-outs

H1	Q1 X X X 4 Q2 1 2 3 4
H2	Q3 1 2 3 4 Q4 1 2 3 4
OT	HCC

Licence no.	Players		No.	Player In	Fouls 1 2 3 4 5
250	MAYER,	F.	0	(X)	Ps
252	MANOS,	J Jr.	3	(X)	
253	JONES,	M	4	X	
254	KENT,	Q.	5		
255	MARTINEZ,	C.	6		
256	LOPEZ,	J. (CAP)	7	(X)	
257	HEMEL,	D.	8		
265	OBRADOVIC,	C.	9		
266	AGUILAR,	V.	10		
268	RIMKUS,	T.	12		
300	PEROTTI,	R.	15	(X)	P1
301	VIDOT,	A.	20	(X)	P2
Head coach	C001 CANUT	J.			
First assistant coach	C80 SERRAT	A.			

Team B CAT BASKET

Time-outs

H1	Q1 X X X 4 Q2 1 2 3 4
H2	Q3 1 2 3 4 Q4 1 2 3 4
OT	HCC

Licence no.	Players		No.	Player In	Fouls 1 2 3 4 5
500	RADONJIC,	G.	4	(X)	P1
501	MANTILA,	P.	5		
502	TANABE,	V.	6	(X)	
503	PUIG,	J.	7		
505	THRON,	H.	8	X	
506	MITLECH,	J.	9	(X)	
700	MARTI,	C.	10		
750	MANJOUR,	R. (CAP)	11	(X)	P
751	TOTEVA,	L	12		
766	LEE,	A.	13		
800	KEM,	B.	14	(X)	P
Head coach	C50 CASTRO	A.			
First assistant coach	C111 AURIENMA	J.M.			

RUNNING SCORE

A	B	A	B	A	B	A	B
1 1		41 41		81 81		121 121	
7 2 2		42 42		82 82		122 122	
3 ● 6		43 43		83 83		123 123	
4 4		44 44		84 84		124 124	
(0) 5 5 8		45 45		85 85		125 125	
6 ● 14		46 46		86 86		126 126	
3 7 8 14		47 47		87 87		127 127	
8 ● 14		48 48		88 88		128 128	
9 9		49 49		89 89		129 129	
(0) 10 10 4		50 50		90 90		130 130	
11 11		51 51		91 91		131 131	
20 12 12 4		52 52		92 92		132 132	
13 13		53 53		93 93		133 133	
14 14 14		54 54		94 94		134 134	
(3) 15 15		55 55		95 95		135 135	
16 16		56 56		96 96		136 136	
17 (17) (14)		57 57		97 97		137 137	
(3) 18 18		58 58		98 98		138 138	
19 19		59 59		99 99		139 139	
20 20		60 60		100 100		140 140	
(4) 21 21		61 61		101 101		141 141	
22 22		62 62		102 102		142 142	
15 23 23		63 63		103 103		143 143	
24 24		64 64		104 104		144 144	
4 (25) 25		65 65		105 105		145 145	
26 26		66 66		106 106		146 146	
27 27		67 67		107 107		147 147	
28 28		68 68		108 108		148 148	
29 29		69 69		109 109		149 149	
30 30		70 70		110 110		150 150	
31 31		71 71		111 111		151 151	
32 32		72 72		112 112		152 152	
33 33		73 73		113 113		153 153	
34 34		74 74		114 114		154 154	
35 35		75 75		115 115		155 155	
36 36		76 76		116 116		156 156	
37 37		77 77		117 117		157 157	
38 38		78 78		118 118		158 158	
39 39		79 79		119 119		159 159	
40 40		80 80		120 120		160 160	

Scorer	ISOLA,	D.
Assistant scorer	ONNA,	M.
Timer	FERNANDEZ,	P.
Shot clock operator	PATTON,	M.

Scores			A	B
Quarter	①	A	25	B 17
Quarter	②	A		B
Quarter	③	A		B
Quarter	④	A		B
Overtimes		A		B

Crew Chief	_____	Final Score	Team A ____	Team B ____
Umpire 1 ____	Umpire 2 ____	Name of winning team		
Captain'signature in case of protest ____		Game ended at (hh:mm)		

4.8.2 第1节结束

国际篮球联合会记录表

A队 BC MIES   **B队** CAT BASKET

| 竞赛名称 | BASCUP 2022 | 日期 | 15.06.23 | 时间 | 20:30 | 主裁判员 | KOTLEBA, L (SVK) |
| 比赛序号 | 169 | 地点 | FIBA ARENA, GENEVE | 副裁判员1 JUNGEBRAND,O (FIN) 副裁判员2 RIGAS,C (GRE) |

A队 BC MIES

暂停 — 全队犯规

上半时: 节1 X 1 2 3 4   节2 1 2 3 4
下半时: 节3 1 2 3 4   节4 1 2 3 4
决胜期: 主教练挑战 ☐

证件号码	队员	号	上场队员	犯规 1 2 3 4 5
250	MAYBR, F.	0	X	P3
252	MANOS, J Jr.	3	X	
253	JONES, M	4	X	
254	KENT, Q	5		☐
255	MARTINEZ, C.	6		
256	LOPEZ, J. (CAP)	7	X	
257	HEMEL, D.	8		
265	OBRADOVIC, C.	9		
266	AGUILAR, V.	10		
268	RIMIKIS, T.	12		
300	PEROTTI, R.	15	X	P1
301	VIDOT, A.	20	X	P2
主教练	C001 CANUT J.			
第一助理教练	C80 SERRAT A.			

B队 CAT BASKET

暂停 — 全队犯规

上半时: 节1 X 1 2 3 4   节2 1 2 3 4
下半时: 节3 1 2 3 4   节4 1 2 3 4
决胜期: 主教练挑战 ☐

证件号码	队员	号	上场队员	犯规 1 2 3 4 5
500	RADONJIC, G.	4	X	P1
501	MANTILA, P.	5		
502	TANABE, V.	6	X	
503	PUIG, J.	7		
505	THRON, H.	8	X	
506	MITLEOH, J.	9	X	
700	MARTI, C.	10		
750	MANJOUR, R. (CAP)	11	X	P
751	TOTEVA, I.	12		
766	LEE, A.	13		
800	KEM, V.	14	X	P
主教练	C50 CASTRO A.			
第一助理教练	C111 AURJENMA J.M.			

记录员	ISOLA, D.
助理记录员	ONNA, M.
计时员	FERNANDEZ, P.
进攻计时员	PATTON, M.

累积分

A	B	A	B	A	B	A	B
1 1		41 41		81 81		121 121	
2 2		42 42		82 82		122 122	
3 3	⓪ 6	43 43		83 83		123 123	
4 4		44 44		84 84		124 124	
⓪ 5	⑤ 8	45 45		85 85		125 125	
6 6	⑥ 14	46 46		86 86		126 126	
3 7	⑦ 14	47 47		87 87		127 127	
8 8	⑦ 14	48 48		88 88		128 128	
9 9	49 49		89 89		129 129	
⓪ 10	10 10	50 50		90 90		130 130	
11 11		51 51		91 91		131 131	
20 12	12 12	52 52		92 92		132 132	
13 13		53 53		93 93		133 133	
14 14	14	54 54		94 94		134 134	
3 15	15 15	55 55		95 95		135 135	
16 16		56 56		96 96		136 136	
17 17	14	57 57		97 97		137 137	
3 18	18 18	58 58		98 98		138 138	
19 19		59 59		99 99		139 139	
20 20		60 60		100 100		140 140	
4 21	21 21	61 61		101 101		141 141	
22 22		62 62		102 102		142 142	
15 23		63 63		103 103		143 143	
24 24		64 64		104 104		144 144	
4 25		65 65		105 105		145 145	
26 26		66 66		106 106		146 146	
27 27		67 67		107 107		147 147	
28 28		68 68		108 108		148 148	
29 29		69 69		109 109		149 149	
30 30		70 70		110 110		150 150	
31 31		71 71		111 111		151 151	
32 32		72 72		112 112		152 152	
33 33		73 73		113 113		153 153	
34 34		74 74		114 114		154 154	
35 35		75 75		115 115		155 155	
36 36		76 76		116 116		156 156	
37 37		77 77		117 117		157 157	
38 38		78 78		118 118		158 158	
39 39		79 79		119 119		159 159	
40 40		80 80		120 120		160 160	

得分

	A	B
节①	A 25	B 17
节②	A	B
节③	A	B
节④	A	B
决胜期	A	B

主裁判员	_____	最后比分	A队 ____	B队 ____
副裁判员1	____ 副裁判员2 ____	胜队 ____	
球队申诉队长签名		比赛结束时间（时：分）	

4.8.3 END OF 2ND QUARTER

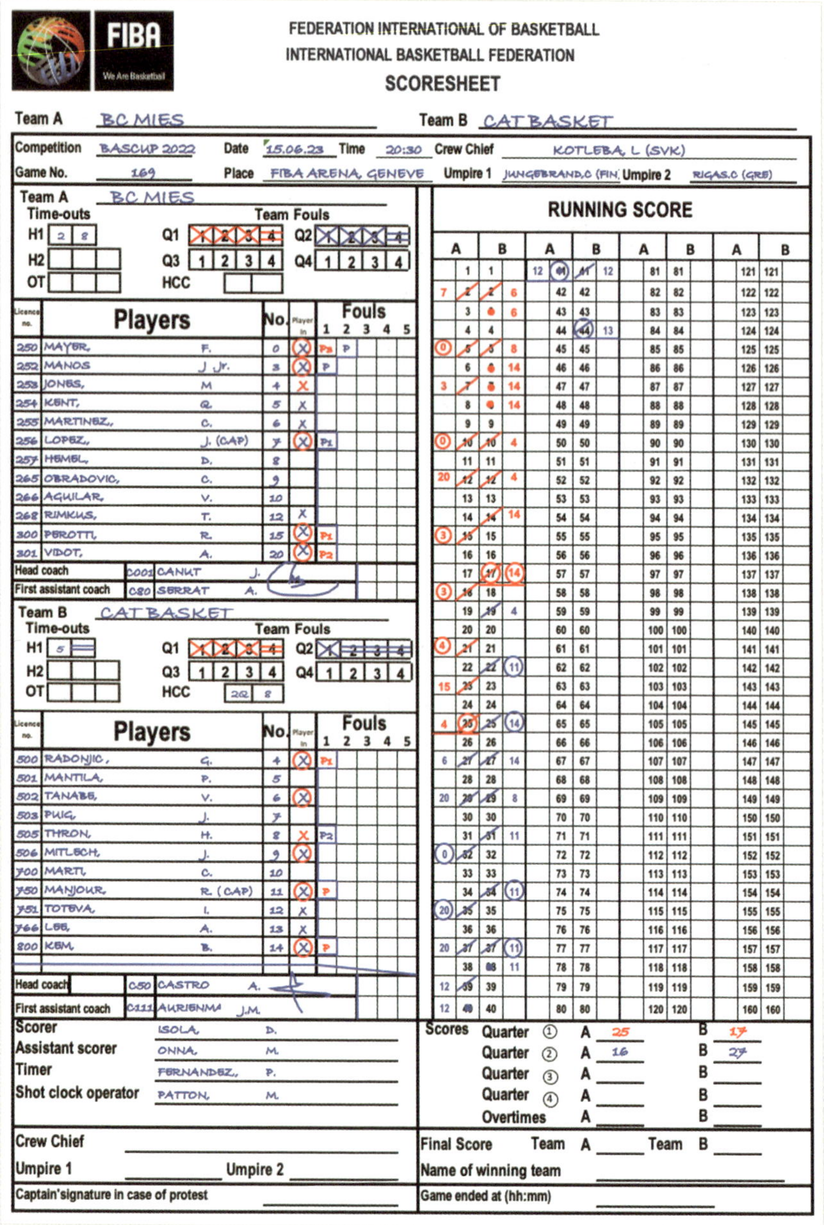

FIBA We Are Basketball

FEDERATION INTERNATIONAL OF BASKETBALL
INTERNATIONAL BASKETBALL FEDERATION
SCORESHEET

Team A BC MIES — Team B CAT BASKET

Competition BASCUP 2022 — Date 15.06.23 — Time 20:30 — Crew Chief KOTLEBA, L (SVK)
Game No. 169 — Place FIBA ARENA, GENEVE — Umpire 1 JUNGEBRAND,C (FIN) — Umpire 2 RIGAS,C (GRE)

Team A BC MIES
Time-outs: H1 2 8 — H2 — OT
Team Fouls: Q1 1 2 3 4 (all crossed) — Q2 1 2 3 4 (all crossed) — Q3 1 2 3 4 — Q4 1 2 3 4 — HCC

Licence no.	Players		No.	Player in	Fouls 1	2	3	4	5
250	MAYER,	F.	0	⊗	P2	P			
252	MANOS	J Jr.	3	⊗	P				
253	JONES,	M	4	X					
254	KENT,	Q.	5	X					
255	MARTINEZ,	C.	6	X					
256	LOPEZ,	J. (CAP)	7	⊗	P1				
257	HEMEL,	D.	8						
265	OBRADOVIC,	C.	9						
266	AGUILAR,	V.	10						
268	RIMKUS,	T.	12	X					
300	PEROTTI,	R.	15	⊗	P1				
301	VIDOT,	A.	20	⊗	P2				
Head coach	C001 CANUT	J.							
First assistant coach	C80 SERRAT	A.							

Team B CAT BASKET
Time-outs: H1 5 — H2 — OT
Team Fouls: Q1 1 2 3 4 (all crossed) — Q2 1 2 3 4 (crossed) — Q3 1 2 3 4 — Q4 1 2 3 4 — HCC 2Q 8

Licence no.	Players		No.	Player in	Fouls 1	2	3	4	5
500	RADONJIC,	G.	4	⊗	P1				
501	MANTILA,	P.	5						
502	TANABE,	V.	6	⊗					
503	PUIG,	J.	7						
505	THRON,	H.	8	X	P2				
506	MITLECH,	J.	9	⊗					
700	MARTI,	C.	10						
750	MANJOUR,	R. (CAP)	11	⊗	P				
751	TOTEVA,	I.	12	X					
766	LEE,	A.	13	X					
800	KEM,	B.	14	⊗	P				
Head coach	C50 CASTRO	A.							
First assistant coach	C111 AURIENMA	J.M.							

RUNNING SCORE

	A	B			A	B		A	B	A	B
	1	1		12	(41)	41/	12	81	81	121	121
7	2/	2/	6		42	42		82	82	122	122
	3	3●	6		43	43		83	83	123	123
	4	4			44	(44)	13	84	84	124	124
(0)	5/	5/	8		45	45		85	85	125	125
	6	6●	14		46	46		86	86	126	126
3	7/	7●	14		47	47		87	87	127	127
	8	8●	14		48	48		88	88	128	128
	9	9			49	49		89	89	129	129
(0)	10/	10/	4		50	50		90	90	130	130
	11	11			51	51		91	91	131	131
20	12/	12/	4		52	52		92	92	132	132
	13	13			53	53		93	93	133	133
	14	14/	14		54	54		94	94	134	134
(3)	15/	15			55	55		95	95	135	135
	16	16			56	56		96	96	136	136
	17	(17)	(14)		57	57		97	97	137	137
(3)	18/	18			58	58		98	98	138	138
	19	19/	4		59	59		99	99	139	139
	20	20			60	60		100	100	140	140
(4)	21/	21			61	61		101	101	141	141
	22	22/	(11)		62	62		102	102	142	142
15	23/	23			63	63		103	103	143	143
	24	24			64	64		104	104	144	144
4	(25)	25/	(14)		65	65		105	105	145	145
	26	26			66	66		106	106	146	146
6	27/	27/	14		67	67		107	107	147	147
	28	28			68	68		108	108	148	148
20	29/	29/	8		69	69		109	109	149	149
	30	30			70	70		110	110	150	150
	31	31/	11		71	71		111	111	151	151
(0)	32/	32			72	72		112	112	152	152
	33	33			73	73		113	113	153	153
	34	34/	(11)		74	74		114	114	154	154
(20)	35/	35			75	75		115	115	155	155
	36	36			76	76		116	116	156	156
20	37/	37/	(11)		77	77		117	117	157	157
	38	38●	11		78	78		118	118	158	158
12	39/	39			79	79		119	119	159	159
12	40●	40			80	80		120	120	160	160

Scorer ISOLA, D.
Assistant scorer ONNA, M.
Timer FERNANDEZ, P.
Shot clock operator PATTON, M.

Scores
Quarter ① A 25 B 17
Quarter ② A 16 B 27
Quarter ③ A ___ B ___
Quarter ④ A ___ B ___
Overtimes A ___ B ___

Crew Chief ___
Umpire 1 ___ Umpire 2 ___
Captain's signature in case of protest ___

Final Score Team A ___ Team B ___
Name of winning team ___
Game ended at (hh:mm) ___

篮球记录台人员手册

4.8.3 第 2 节结束

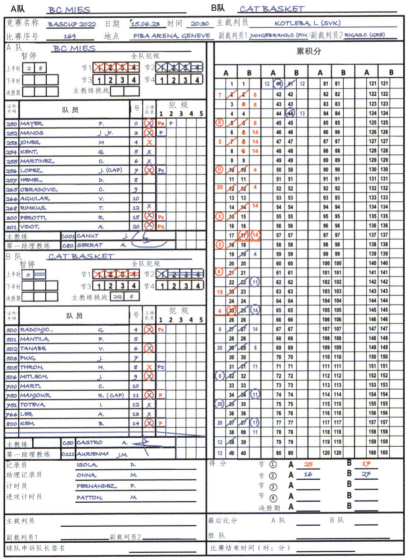

4.8.4 END OF 3RD QUARTER

FEDERATION INTERNATIONAL OF BASKETBALL
INTERNATIONAL BASKETBALL FEDERATION
SCORESHEET

Team A BC MIES

Team B CAT BASKET

Competition	BASCUP 2022	Date	15.06.23	Time	20:30	Crew Chief	KOTLEBA, L (SVK)
Game No.	169	Place	FIBA ARENA, GENEVE	Umpire 1	JUNGEBRAND,O (FIN)	Umpire 2	RIGAS,O (GRE)

Team A BC MIES

Time-outs

H1	2 8	Q1	Q2	
H2	9	Q3	Q4	1 2 3 4
OT		HCC	3Q 5	

Licence no.	Players		No.	Player in	Fouls 1 2 3 4 5
250	MAYER,	F.	0		⊗ P2 P P
252	MANOS,	J. Jr.	3		⊗ P P
253	JONES,	M.	4		X
254	KENT,	G.	5		X
255	MARTINEZ,	C.	6		X P2
256	LOPEZ,	J. (CAP)	7		⊗ P2
257	HEMEL,	D.	8		
265	OBRADOVIC,	C.	9		
266	AGUILAR,	V.	10		
268	RIMKUS,	T.	12		X
300	PEROTTI,	R.	15		⊗ P2
301	VIDOT,	A.	20		⊗ P2 P2

Head coach C001 CANUT J.
First assistant coach C20 SERRAT A.

Team B CAT BASKET

Time-outs

H1	5	Q1	Q2	
H2	5	Q3	Q4	1 2 3 4
OT		HCC	2Q 8	

Licence no.	Players		No.	Player in	Fouls 1 2 3 4 5
500	RADONJIC,	G.	4		⊗ P2 P
501	MANTILA,	P.	5		
502	TANABE,	V.	6		⊗
503	PUIG,	J.	7		
505	THRON,	H.	8		X P2
506	MITLECH,	J.	9		⊗ P2 P
700	MARTI,	C.	10		
750	MANJOUR,	R. (CAP)	11		⊗ P U2
751	TOTEVA,	L.	12		X
766	LEE,	A.	13		X P2 P2
800	KEM,	B.	14		⊗ P

Head coach C50 CASTRO A.
First assistant coach C111 AURIBNMA JM.

Scorer	ISOLA,	D.
Assistant scorer	ONNA,	M.
Timer	FERNANDEZ,	P.
Shot clock operator	PATTON,	M.

RUNNING SCORE

A	B	A	B	A	B	A	B
1	1	12 44 41 12	81 81	121 121
7 7 6	42 42	82 82	122 122
3 6	43 43	83 83	123 123
4 4	44 44 13	84 84	124 124
0 5 8 0	45 45	85 85	125 125
6 14	46 46 14	86 86	126 126
3 7 8 14 3	47 47	87 87	127 127
8 14	48 48	88 88	128 128
9 9 15	49 49	89 89	129 129
0 10 10 4	50 50 11	90 90	130 130
11 11	51 51	91 91	131 131
20 12 12 4 7	52 52 9	92 92	132 132
13 13	53 53	93 93	133 133
14 14 14	54 54	94 94	134 134
3 15 15 20 55 55 11	95 95	135 135
16 16	56 56	96 96	136 136
17 17 14 0 57 57	97 97	137 137
3 18 18 6 58 58	98 98	138 138
19 19 4 6 59 59 5	99 99	139 139
20 20	60 60 5	100 100	140 140
4 21 21 3 61 61	101 101	141 141
22 22 11	62 62	102 102	142 142
15 23 23 6 63 63 8	103 103	143 143
24 24	64 64	104 104	144 144
4 25 25 14 20 65 65 11	105 105	145 145
26 26	66 66	106 106	146 146
6 27 27 14	67 67	107 107	147 147
28 28	68 68 13	108 108	148 148
20 29 29 8	69 69	109 109	149 149
30 30	70 70 9	110 110	150 150
31 31 11	71 71 9	111 111	151 151
0 32 32	72 72	112 112	152 152
33 33	73 73	113 113	153 153
34 34 11	74 74 11	114 114	154 154
20 35 35	75 75	115 115	155 155
36 36	76 76	116 116	156 156
20 37 37 11	77 77	117 117	157 157
38 38 11	78 78	118 118	158 158
12 39 39	79 79	119 119	159 159
12 40 40	80 80	120 120	160 160

Scores	Quarter		A	B
	Quarter	①	A 25	B 17
	Quarter	②	A 16	B 27
	Quarter	③	A 24	B 30
	Quarter	④	A ___	B ___
	Overtimes		A ___	B ___

Crew Chief	_____	Final Score	Team A ___	Team B ___
Umpire 1	___ Umpire 2 ___	Name of winning team	_____	
Captain'signature in case of protest	_____	Game ended at (hh:mm)	_____	

4.8.4 第3节结束

国际篮球联合会记录表

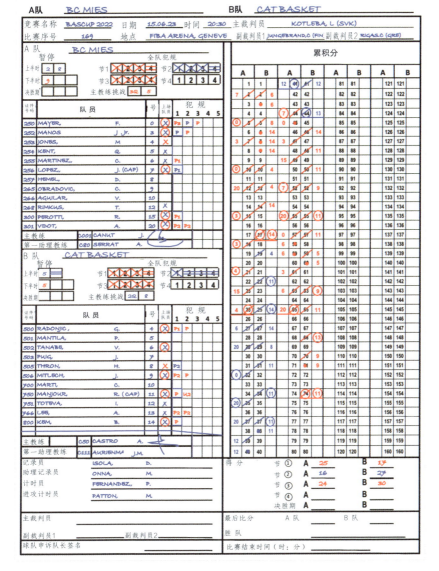

4.8.5 END OF 4TH QUARTER

FEDERATION INTERNATIONAL OF BASKETBALL
INTERNATIONAL BASKETBALL FEDERATION

SCORESHEET

Team A BC MIES   Team B CAT BASKET

Competition	BASCUP 2022	Date	15.06.23	Time	20:30	Crew Chief	KOTLEBA, L (SVK)
Game No.	169	Place	FIBA ARENA, GENEVE	Umpire 1	JUNGEBRAND,C (FIN	Umpire 2	RIGAS,C (GRE)

Team A BC MIES

Time-outs
H1 2 8   Q1 ☒☒☒☒ Q2 ☒☒☒☒☒
H2 9 10 10   Q3 ☒☒☒☒ Q4 ☒☒☒☒
OT ___   HCC 3Q 5

Licence no.	Players		No.	Player in	Fouls 1	2	3	4	5
250	MAYER,	F.	0	☒	P₁	P	P		
252	MANOS	J. Jr.	3	☒	P	P			
253	JONES,	M	4	X					
254	KENT,	R.	5	X					
255	MARTINEZ,	O.	6	X	P₁				
256	LOPEZ,	J. (CAP)	7	☒	P₁	P			
257	HEMEL,	D.	8						
265	OBRADOVIC,	O.	9						
266	AGUILAR,	V.	10						
268	RIMKUS,	T.	12	X					
300	PEROTTI,	R.	15	☒	P₁	P₂	P	P₂	
301	VIDOT,	A.	20	☒	P₂	P₃	P		

Head coach 0001 CANUT J. Co
First assistant coach C80 SERRAT A.

Team B CAT BASKET

Time-outs
H1 5   Q1 ☒☒☒☒ Q2 ☒☒☒☒
H2 5 6 10   Q3 ☒☒☒☒ Q4 ☒☒☒☒
OT ___   HCC 2Q 8

Licence no.	Players		No.	Player in	Fouls 1	2	3	4	5
500	RADONJIC,	G.	4	☒	P₁	P			
501	MANTILA,	P.	5						
502	TANABE,	V.	6	☒	P				
503	PUIG,	J.	7						
505	THRON,	H.	8	X	P₂				
506	MITLECH,	J.	9	☒	P₂	P	P₁		
700	MARTI,	O.	10						
750	MANJOUR,	R. (CAP)	11	☒	P	U2	P₃	P₂	
751	TOTEVA,	L.	12	X					
766	LEE,	A.	13	X	P₂	P₂			
800	KEM,	B.	14	☒	P	P			

Head coach C50 CASTRO A.
First assistant coach C111 AURIENMA J.M.

Scorer	ISOLA,	D.
Assistant scorer	ONNA,	M.
Timer	FERNANDEZ,	P.
Shot clock operator	PATTON,	M.

RUNNING SCORE

(running score columns A/B from 1 to 160)

Scores		A		B	
Quarter	①	A	25	B	17
Quarter	②	A	16	B	27
Quarter	③	A	24	B	30
Quarter	④	A	27	B	16
Overtimes		A		B	

Crew Chief _____
Umpire 1 _____ Umpire 2 _____
Captain'signature in case of protest _____

Final Score Team A ___ Team B ___
Name of winning team _____
Game ended at (hh:mm) _____

4.8.5 第4节结束

国际篮球联合会记录表

A队 _BC MIES_   B队 _CAT BASKET_

竞赛名称 _BASCUP 2022_	日期 _15.06.23_ 时间 _20:30_	主裁判员 _KOTLEBA, L (SVK)_
比赛序号 _169_	地点 _FIBA ARENA, GENEVE_	副裁判员1 _JUNGEBRAND,C (FIN)_ 副裁判员2 _RIGAS,C (GRE)_

A队 _BC MIES_

暂停
上半时 `2` `8`
下半时 `9` `10` `10`
决胜期

全队犯规
节1 ✗✗✗4 节2 ✗✗3 4
节3 ✗✗3 4 节4 ✗✗✗4

主教练挑战 `3Q` `5`

证件号码	队员		号	上场队员	犯规 1 2 3 4 5
250	MAYER,	F.	0	Ⓧ	P5 P P
252	MANOS,	J. Jr.	3		P P
253	JONES,	M.	4	Ⓧ	
254	KENT,	Q.	5	X	
255	MARTINEZ,	C.	6	X	P1
256	LOPEZ,	J. (CAP)	7	Ⓧ	P1 P
257	HEMEL,	D.	8		
265	OBRADOVIC,	C.	9		
266	AGUILAR,	V.	10		
268	RIMKUS,	T.	12	X	
300	PEROTTI,	R.	15	Ⓧ	P1 P2 P2
301	VIDOT,	A.	20	Ⓧ	P2 P2 P

主教练 _C001 CANUT J._ Co
第一助理教练 _C20 SERRAT A._

B队 _CAT BASKET_

暂停
上半时 `5`
下半时 `5` `6` `10`
决胜期

全队犯规
节1 ✗✗✗4 节2 ✗✗3 4
节3 ✗✗3 4 节4 ✗✗✗4

主教练挑战 `2Q` `8`

证件号码	队员		号	上场队员	犯规 1 2 3 4 5
500	RADONJIC,	G.	4		P1 P
501	MANTILA,	P.	5		
502	TANABE,	V.	6	Ⓧ	P
503	PUIG,	J.	7		
505	THRON,	H.	8	X	P2
506	MILBON,	J.	9	Ⓧ	P2 P P1
700	MARTI,	C.	10		
750	MANJOUR,	R. (CAP)	11	Ⓧ	H2 P3 P2
751	TOTEVA,	I.	12	X	
766	LEE,	A.	13	X	P
800	KIM,	B.	14	Ⓧ	P P

主教练 _C50 CASTRO A._ Co
第一助理教练 _C111 AURIENMA J.M._

记录员	_ISOLA, D._	
助理记录员	_ONNA, M._	
计时员	_FERNANDEZ, P._	
进攻计时员	_PATTON, M._	

累积分

(累积分栏 A/B 1–160)

得分	节	A		B
	①	25		17
	②	16		27
	③	24		30
	④	27		16
	决胜期	A		B

最后比分 A队   B队
胜队

主裁判员
副裁判员1   副裁判员2
球队申诉队长签名   比赛结束时间（时：分）

4.8.6 END OF THE GAME

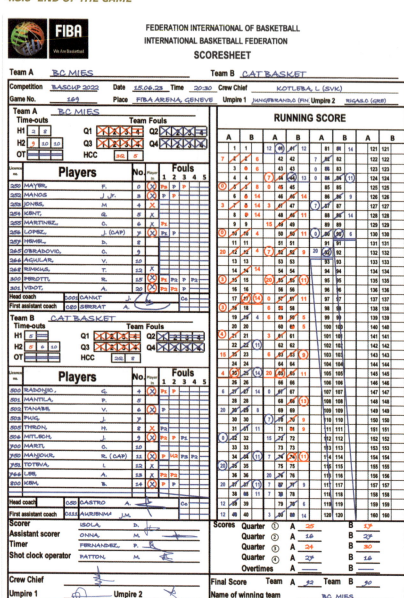

篮球记录台人员手册

4.8.6 比赛结束

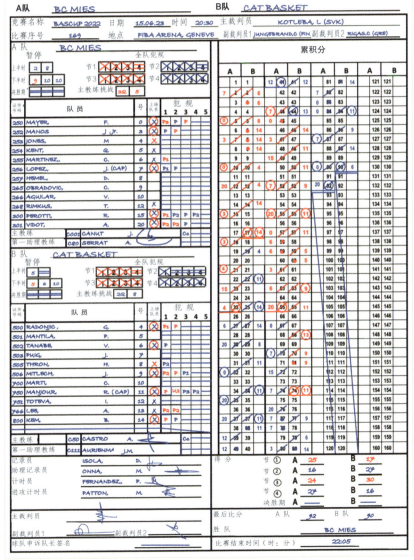

4.8.7 END OF OVERTIME

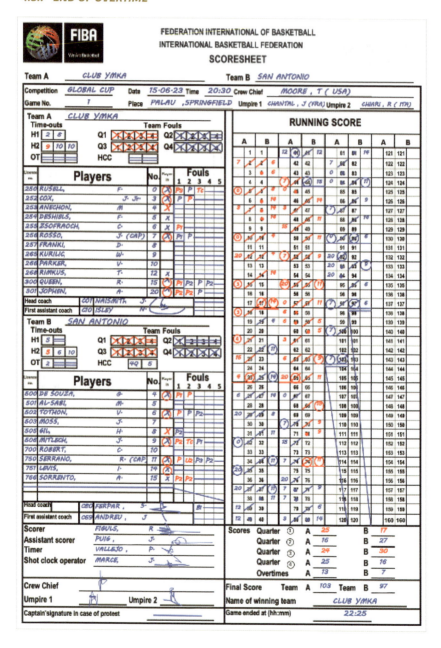

4.8.7 决胜期结束

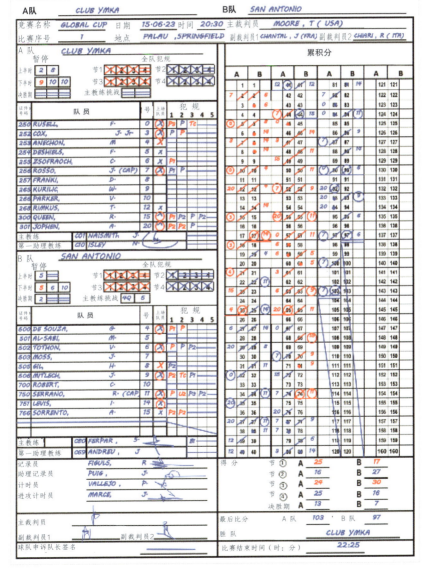

4.9 ALTERNATING POSSESSION ARROW

Alternating possession is a method of causing the ball to become live with a throw-in rather than a jump ball. In all jump ball situations (except at the start of a game) teams will alternate possession of the ball for a throw-in at the place nearest to where the jump ball situation occurs.

4.9.1 POSITIONING THE ALTERNATING POSSESSION ARROW

The team that does not gain control of the live ball after the jump ball will be entitled to the first alternating possession. For example, if team A gains possession of the ball from the opening jump ball, the direction arrow will point towards the basket that team B will be shooting into.

The team entitled to the next alternating possession at the end of any quarter shall start the next quarter with a throw-in at the centre line extended, opposite the scorer's table, unless there are further free throws and a possession penalty to be administered.

If **control of a live ball** has not yet been established, the Table Official cannot use the alternating possession arrow to award possession.

This means that if in an opening jump ball the ball is legally tapped by jumper A1 and then a held ball or a double foul between A2 and B2 is called, the referee shall administer another jump ball in the centre circle and A2 and B2 shall jump. Whatever time has passed on the game clock, after the ball is legally tapped, and before the held ball/double foul situation, shall remain consumed. Similarly, if the tipped ball at the start of the game is tapped directly out of bounds, then the scorer must wait until one of the teams has gained possession of the ball for the throw-in before placing the directional arrow.

The team entitled to the alternating possession throw-in shall be indicated by the alternating possession arrow in the direction of the opponents' basket.

This means that after the jump ball if a player/team gains control of the ball, the alternating possession arrow shall point to the basket in the opposite direction of play. For example, if team A gains control and their direction of play is towards the right basket, then the alternating possession arrow shall point towards the left basket.

4.9 交替拥有箭头

交替拥有是以掷球入界而不是以跳球来使球成活球的一种方法。在所有的跳球情况中（开始比赛的跳球除外），双方球队应交替拥有从最靠近发生跳球情况的地点掷球入界。

4.9.1 交替拥有程序

跳球后未首先获得控制活球的球队将拥有第一次交替拥有掷球入界权。例如：A 队在开始比赛的跳球中获得了球权，那么交替拥有箭头将要指向B 队进攻方向。

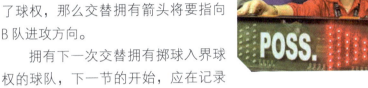

拥有下一次交替拥有掷球入界球权的球队，下一节的开始，应在记录台对侧的中线延长线处，掷球入界开始比赛，除非还有更进一步的包含罚球和掷球入界的罚则需要执行。

如果球队在场上还没有清晰地**控制活球**，那么记录台人员不能翻转交替拥有箭头。

这意味着，如果在开始比赛的跳球中，A1 合法拍击了球，紧接着发生了 A2 和 B2 的争球，那么，裁判员应当宣判 A2 和 B2 在中线位置进行一次新的跳球。球在被合法拍击后至发生争球或双方犯规之前，无论经过了多少时间，都要保留交替拥有箭头。同样，如果在开始比赛的跳球中，球在被合法拍击后出界了，那么记录员必须在新的球队在掷球入界的队员可处理球时，立即翻转交替拥有箭头。

应由指向对方球篮的交替拥有箭头来指明拥有交替拥有掷球入界球权的球队。

这意味着，在跳球后，如果一名队员或球队在场上获得了控制球，那么交替拥有箭头应指向获得控制球队的本方球篮。例如：如果 A 队获得了控制球，向场地右侧的球篮进攻，那么交替拥有箭头将指向场地左侧的球篮。

If the referee tosses the ball for the opening jump ball and, immediately after the ball is legally tapped by a jumper the ball goes directly out-of-bounds, or is caught by one of the jumpers before it has touched one of the non-jumpers or the floor, this is a violation.

In both cases the opponents are awarded a throw-in as the result of the violation.

The team that does not get the throw-in will be entitled to the first alternating possession at the place nearest to where the next jump ball situation occurs.

4.9.2   OPERATING THE ALTERNATING POSSESSION ARROW

The direction of the alternating possession arrow is reversed immediately when the alternating possession throw-in ends.

Alternating possession:

- **Begins** when the ball is at the disposal of the player taking the throw-in.
- **Ends** when:
    - The ball touches or is legally touched by any player on the playing court.
    - The team taking the throw-in commits a violation.
    - A live ball lodges between the ring and the backboard during a throw-in.

A violation by a team during its alternating possession throw-in causes that team to lose the alternating possession throw-in.

The direction of the alternating possession arrow will be reversed immediately, indicating that the opponents of the violating team will be entitled to the alternating possession throw-in at the next jump ball situation. The game shall then be resumed by awarding the ball to the opponents of the violating team for a throw-in at the place of the original throw-in.

A foul by either team:

- Before the beginning of a quarter other than the first quarter, or
- during the alternating possession throw-in,

does not cause the team entitled to the throw-in to lose that alternating possession.

Should such a foul occur during the initial throw-in to start a quarter, after the ball has been placed at the disposal of the player taking the throw-in, but before it has legally touched a player on the playing court, the alternating possession procedure has not ended therefore the arrow stays pointing in the same direction.

如果开场跳球时，球在离开裁判员的手后，在跳球队员合法拍击后直接出界了；或跳球队员在球触及其他非跳球队员或地面之前直接控制了球，这是一起违例。

在这两个案例中，应判给对方球队由于跳球违例而带来的掷球入界。

掷球入界后，没有在场上获得控制活球的球队，将在下一次发生跳球情况的就近地点获得交替拥有掷球入界球权。

4.9.2 操作交替拥有箭头

在交替拥有的掷球入界完成后，交替拥有指示箭头立即反转。

交替拥有程序：

- **开始**于：掷球入界队员可处理球时。
- **结束**于：
  - 球触及场上队员或被场上队员合法触及时。
  - 掷球入界队发生违例时。
  - 掷球入界中活球夹在篮圈和篮板之间时。

某队在它的交替拥有掷球入界中违例，使该队失掉交替拥有掷球入界球权。

交替拥有箭头应立即反转，指明违例队的对方拥有下一次跳球情况中的交替拥有掷球入界球权。于是将球判给违例队的对方在最初的掷球入界地点掷球入界继续比赛。

任一球队犯规，发生在：

- 除第一节以外的任一节比赛开始之前，或
- 交替拥有掷球入界过程中，

任一球队犯规不使掷球入界队失掉交替拥有掷球入界球权。

开始一节比赛的掷球入界时，在掷球入界队员可处理球以后至球被场上队员合法触及之前，交替拥有箭头应当保持指向原有方向。

If a held ball is called by a referee and the scorer makes an error and the ball is erroneously awarded to a wrong team for the throw-in, once the ball touches or is legally touched by a player on the playing court, the error cannot be corrected. However, the disadvantaged team shall not lose its alternating possession throw-in opportunity as a result of the error and will be entitled to the next alternating possession throw-in.

Most common situation for alternating possession arrow is the initial jump ball.

Initial jump ball

Team white gains control of the ball.
Possession arrow for team red.

When should the scorer change the direction of the alternating possession arrow?

The scorer shall change the direction every time the ball touches or is legally touched by a player on the playing court, after a throw-in caused by a jump ball situation.

Jump ball situation

Ball legally touched on court   Change

如果裁判员宣判了一起争球情况，但记录员错误地指示了交替拥有的方向，一旦球接触任一场上队员或被任一场上队员合法接触，该失误就不能被纠正了。但是，因为该失误失利的球队不应就该失误而失去在下一次跳球情况发生时交替拥有掷球入界的权利。

建立交替拥有箭头，多数都发生在开场跳球时。

开场跳球   白队在场上控制球，箭头指向红队进攻方向

记录员应何时反转交替拥有箭头？

在交替拥有掷球入界后，当球接触一名场上队员或被一名场上队员合法触及时，记录员应当反转交替拥有箭头。

跳球情况   球被场上队员合法触及   反转箭头

The scorer also shall change the direction of the alternating possession arrow when, after a jump ball situation, the team awarded the throw-in commits a violation during the procedure.

Jump ball situation

Throw-in violation

Change

The scorer shall turn the possession arrow immediately at the beginning of the half-time, and the referees (and the Commissioner if present), are to be notified of this.

When the scorer shall not change the direction of the alternating possession arrow.

A foul by either team:

- before the beginning of a quarter other than the first quarter, or
- during the alternating possession throw-in,

does not cause the team entitled to the throw-in to lose that alternating possession.
In this case, regardless of the penalty, the alternating possession arrow does not change.

Jump ball situation

Foul before the ball is legally on the court

Do not change

在一次跳球情况发生后，当被判给掷球入界的球队在执行程序期间发生违例，记录员应当反转交替拥有箭头。

跳球情况　　　　　　掷球入界违例　　　　　　　　　　反转箭头

记录员应当在半时休息时间开始时反转交替拥有箭头，并提醒裁判员（和到场的技术代表）。

记录员不应反转交替拥有箭头的情况。

任一球队犯规发生在：

- 除第一节以外任一节比赛开始前，或
- 在交替拥有掷球入界过程中，

不使该球队失去原有的交替拥有权利。

在这些情况下，无论罚则如何，交替拥有箭头不变。

跳球情况　　在球被合法掷入场地前发生犯规　　　　　不反转箭头

When the alternating possession arrow is an electronic device, it shall:

- Have an arrow of a minimum length of 100 mm and a height of 100 mm.

- Display an arrow on the front, illuminated in a bright red colour when switched on, showing the direction of the alternating possession.

- Display on the back side a LED that indicates the left/right/neutral position to verify the correct position.

- Be positioned in the centre of the scorer's table and shall be clearly visible to everyone involved in the game, including the spectators.

4.10 MECHANICS AND PERFORMANCE STANDARDS

To perform their specific task, the scorer shall:

- Complete the scoresheet according to the rules and the Table Officials' Manual.

- Know the referees' signals and mechanics so as to communicate with them effectively.

- Write on the scoresheet the number of player who scored the field goal.

- In case of a fight, make a note of the players (numbers) that may be involved in it. During all fighting situations, the scorer shall observe carefully what happens on the playing court, along with the timer and the Commissioner (if present).

- Pay attention to the referee's signals during three-point attempts. It is the referee who will make the decision on shot attempts taken from close to the three-point line.

- Each time points are scored, call out loudly all relevant information (e.g. 11A, 2 points), and confirm at the same time the score reached (66 – 56 always in the order A-B); to help check that the visible scoreboard is accurate. If there are no differences between the scoresheet and scoreboard the assistant scorer will give verbal confirmation.

- If there is a discrepancy, and the score in scoresheet is correct, the scorer shall immediately take steps to have the scoreboard corrected. If in doubt or if one of the teams raises an objection to the correction, the scorer shall inform the referee as soon as the ball becomes dead and the game clock is stopped.

当交替拥有指示箭头是电子设备时，应当：

- 其箭头的最小长度为 100 毫米，最小高度为 100 毫米。
- 该设备前部安装显示设备，使用鲜亮的红色指示现有的交替拥有进攻方向。
- 该设备后部安装 LED 显示设备，指示交替拥有箭头向左、向右、中立的位置，以验证位置是否正确。
- 它应被放置在记录台的中间位置，使包括观众在内的所有比赛参与者都能够清晰地看到时间信息。

4.10 工作方法及规范

为了规范记录台的工作，记录员应当：

- 根据规则和记录台人员手册的规定完成记录表的填写。
- 知晓裁判员手势和裁判法，以达成高效的交流。
- 在记录表上登记得分队员的号码。
- 如果发生打架情况，记录参与的队员（号码）。在打架情况中，记录员应当与计时员和到场的技术代表一起，细心地观察比赛场地上发生的情况。
- 当出现 3 分试投时，记录员要注意观察裁判员的手势。如果试投位置贴近 3 分线，应由裁判员决定中篮的分值。
- 每当出现得分时，记录员应当大声读出相应信息（例如：A11 得 2 分），同时确认场上比分（66：56，A 队在前），协助检查记录屏的分数是否正确。如果记录表和记录屏上的分数一致，助理记录员要给出口头信号以确认。
- 如果分数出现差异，且记录表上的分数正确时，记录员应当立即采取行动修正记录屏的分数。如果存疑或某一球队对该错误表示质疑，记录员应趁下一次停表的死球机会通知裁判员。

- Each time a foul is called, the scorer shall call out loud all relevant information (e.g. 26 A personal foul, 2 free throws), as reported by the referee. The information shall then be recorded on the scoresheet and the number of personal fouls and team fouls called out (e.g. 26A, 2nd personal foul, 4th team foul, 4 -1 team fouls). The assistant scorer will verbally confirm this and then update the visible scoreboard.

- Quickly inform the rest of the Table Officials, especially the timer, when a player reaches the fifth foul, or must be disqualified as a consequence of the sum of technical and/or unsportsmanlike fouls.

- It is good practice to repeat loudly the player's number and team fouls in situations leading to possible substitutions (3rd or 4th fouls), 5th foul or bonus shots, in order that the table officiating team are vigilant for substitutions, time-outs or the need to place team foul markers on the table.

- Shall listen carefully for comments from colleagues about time-out and substitution requests.

- Once a team has used all of its permitted time-outs during a half (or during overtimes), inform the nearest referee of this clearly, so that this can be communicated to the relevant coach.

- Know the alternating possession rule and when necessary, change the direction of the arrow efficiently.

- Maintain eye contact with referees.

- 每当裁判员宣判犯规时，记录员应当大声读出相应信息（例如：A26个人犯规，2次罚球），此过程应与裁判员的报告同步。随后，记录员应当记录和读出犯规队员的信息、个人犯规次数、全队犯规次数（例如：A26，2次个人犯规；4次全队犯规；A队与B队全队犯规次数4：1）。助理记录员应口头确认，并更新记录屏的信息。

- 当队员出现5次个人犯规而出局或由于累计技术犯规和/或违反体育运动精神的犯规被取消比赛资格时，记录员应当快速完成与记录台人员的沟通，尤其要告知计时员。

- 口语重述犯规队员的号码和全队犯规次数是好的工作技巧，它可以让记录台人员警惕和妥善应对在队员个人第3次、4次、5次犯规或全队犯规处罚状态罚球时，可能带来的替换、暂停和摆放全队犯规处罚状态标识的情况。

- 应注意听同伴关于暂停和替换的申请。

- 每半时（或决胜期），当某一球队使用了全部暂停次数时，记录员应当向就近的裁判员清晰地告知这一信息，以便于裁判员向教练员传达这一信息。

- 知晓交替拥有程序的规则，当需要时，高效地操作交替拥有箭头。

- 保持与裁判员的眼神交流。

第 5 章

THE ASSISTANT SCORER

助理记录员

THE ASSISTANT SCORER

5.1 ASSISTANT SCORER'S DUTIES

The assistant scorer shall operate the scoreboard and constantly assist the scorer and timer. In the case of any discrepancy between the scoreboard and the scoresheet which cannot be resolved, the scoresheet shall take precedence and the scoreboard shall be corrected accordingly.

5.2 BEFORE THE GAME SCOREBOARD

Scoreboard

The scoreboard should be clearly visible to everyone involved in the game, including the spectators. In case television or video displays are used it must be assured that the complete required information shall be visible at any time during the game. The readability of the displayed information shall be identical compared to that of a digital scoreboard.

The scoreboard shall include and/or indicate:

- The digital countdown game clock and have the ability to indicate time remaining in minutes and seconds, as well as tenths (1/10) of a second only during the last minute of the quarter.
- The points scored by each team.
- The teams' names.

助理记录员

5.1 助理记录员的职责

助理记录员应操作记录屏并持续为记录员提供协助。任何关于记录表和记录屏记录数据不统一的情况，都应当以记录表为准，根据记录表修正记录屏的数据。

5.2 赛前

记录屏

记录屏应使包括观众在内的所有比赛参与者能够清晰地看到时间信息。如果有电视信号和视频，必须保证在比赛过程中显示比赛规定的信息。显示信息清晰易读，应当与数字记录屏一致，便于辨别。

记录屏应当包括和 / 或显示以下信息：

- 倒计时的计时钟，能够显示剩余时间的分钟和秒，在每节比赛的最后 1 分钟，能够显示 1/10 秒的计时单位。
- 双方球队得分。
- 双方球队名称。

- The number of team fouls from 1 to 5, stopping at 5 (if possible).

- The number of the quarter from 1 to 4, and E for an overtime.

- The number of charged time-outs per half from 0 to 3.

- For FIBA Level 1 games, the surname and number of each player (at least twelve player 'slots' should be available to show all players) and the cumulative points scored and fouls by each player.

- A display clock for timing the time-outs (optional). The game clock must not be used for this purpose.

The assistant scorer must check the equipment to verify it works correctly. In particular, it must be checked if all LEDs or characters on the scoreboard work correctly. If there is a malfunction with any of the LEDs or characters on the scoreboard, the Crew Chief and/or the Commissioner (if present) should be notified.

The assistant scorer should check the following:

- If the game clock is electronically linked to the shot clock or not.

- Verify LEDs or characters on the scoreboard - setting displays to 888 (if possible).

- Check to see if team foul totals can be stopped at 5.

- If the quarter numbers can be changed manually.

- If the number of time-outs can be changed manually.

- How to reset fouls and time-outs during intervals (if this reset is not automatic).

- How to correct players' scores in case of an error (i.e. add and cancel points).

- How to correct fouls in case of an error.

- How the time on the game clock can be corrected (seconds and / or tenths of a second (in the last minute) added on or taken off).

- If there is a button on the console to sound an audible signal.

- 1~5 次全队犯规次数，在 5 次时终止（如可能的话）。
- 1~4 的节次信息，决胜期显示 E。
- 显示每半时 0~3 次的已请求暂停次数。
- 国际篮联的一级比赛中，显示每位队员的姓氏和号码（至少显示 12 名队员），个人累计得分和个人犯规次数。
- 一个用来显示计量暂停时间的计时钟。比赛计时钟不能用于此目的。

助理记录员必须检查所使用的设备能否正确运行。特别是，必须测试记录屏上所有的 LED 灯或字符是否可以正确运行，如果记录屏上的任一 LED 灯或字符出现故障，应通知主裁判和 / 或到场的技术代表。

助理记录员应当按照如下顺序检查：

- 比赛计时钟与进攻计时钟的电子信号是否相连。
- 检查记录屏的 LED 灯或字符，设置成显示"888"（如可能的话）。
- 检查全队犯规次数能否显示至 5 次。
- 检查节次信息能否被手动设置。
- 检查暂停次数能否被手动设置。
- 比赛休息期如何重置犯规和暂停次数（如果这些不是自动重置的话）。
- 出现失误时如何修改队员的个人得分（加减分）。
- 出现失误时如何修改队员的个人犯规。
- 如何修改比赛计时钟上的时间[秒和 / 或 1/10 秒（最后 1 分钟），时间加减]。
- 检查是否有开启声音信号的按钮。

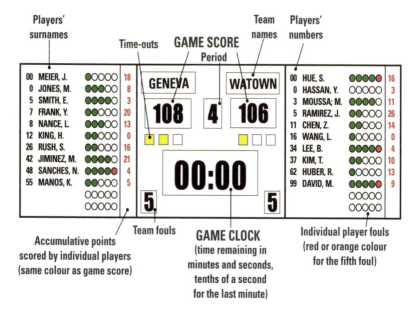

Players' surnames | Time-outs | GAME SCORE Period | Team names | Players' numbers

Accumulative points scored by individual players (same colour as game score) — Team fouls — GAME CLOCK (time remaining in minutes and seconds, tenths of a second for the last minute) — Individual player fouls (red or orange colour for the fifth foul)

5.3 DURING THE GAME

How to update the scoreboard

- Records on the scoreboard shall be the same as the scoresheet. Team fouls shall be stopped when they reach the fifth foul (if possible).

How to collaborate with the scorer

- The assistant scorer shall report in order, the player's number, team, and points scored (e.g. 14B, 2 points);

- The scorer states the running score in the following order: the team that has just scored, then the game score, in A–B format (e.g. 40, 57–40);

- The assistant scorer repeats the score to confirm whether the running score on the scoreboard is correct.

- It is important that this is loud enough for the Commissioner (if present) to hear and to also check.

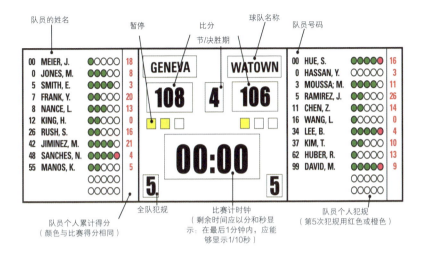

队员的姓名　暂停　比分　球队名称　队员号码

节/决胜期

队员个人累计得分
（颜色与比赛得分相同）

全队犯规

比赛计时钟
（剩余时间应以分和秒显
示：在最后1分钟内，应能
够显示1/10秒）

队员个人犯规
（第5次犯规用红色或橙色）

5.3 赛中

如何更新记录屏的信息

- 记录屏的信息应当与记录表保持一致。全队犯规在达到 5 次后，就停止继续累积（如可能的话）。

如何与记录员配合

- 助理记录员应当按此顺序报告：队员号码，球队，得分分值（例如：14 号，B 队，得 2 分）。

- 记录员应当按照如下顺序陈述累积分：得分球队的分值，然后是 A 队与 B 队的比分（例如：40，57：40）。

- 助理记录员应当重述比分，以确定记录表和记录屏的比分是一致的。

- 声音的大小，以到场的技术代表能够清楚地听到并检查为宜，这点很重要。

It is important to note that the assistant scorer must wait until the scorer has confirmed the new score before updating the scoreboard, because the scoresheet shall take precedence over the scoreboard, and not the opposite.

Recording Fouls

- The assistant scorer shall report the player's number, the team, the type of foul, and the penalty (e.g. 14 B, personal, two free throws).

- At the same time that the scorer records it on the scoresheet, the personal foul is confirmed, as well as the total team fouls of the team whose player has just committed the foul, and team fouls situation for both teams in the A-B format (e.g. first personal, third team, 2-3 team fouls);

- The assistant scorer replies 'OK' or 'yes' if the scoreboard is correct.

In this way, the Table Officials have an awareness of foul situation for both teams and individual players. This will help the Table Officials team to anticipate situations such as possible substitutions (eg. 3rd player foul in the first half or 4th player foul early in the game).

Other duties

- The assistant scorer shall also check to see if players who have requested substitutions are eligible to play. Good communication from the timer and shot clock operator about team substitutions is essential for this.

- The assistant scorer may call a time-out or a substitution, if the scorer or timer are busy.

- The assistant scorer has the responsibility for the team bench area to the right of the table in fighting or bench clearance situations.

- The assistant scorer shall help the timer by positioning the team foul marker in the correct place on their side of the table.

5.4 INTERVALS OF PLAY

Cross check with the scorer all key information regarding scores, fouls and time-outs.

Observe the players and bench personnel and inform the referee of any incidents.

同样重要的是，助理记录员必须等到记录员已经确认了新的比分以后，再更新记录屏的信息，因为记录表权威性高于记录屏，而不是相反的。

记录犯规

- 助理记录员应当口头报告犯规队员的号码、球队、犯规类型和罚则（例如： 14号，B队，个人犯规，2次罚球）。

- 与此同时，记录员将其记录在记录表上，记录员需要确认个人犯规次数、全队犯规次数、双方球队犯规次数，顺序采用A∶B的格式（例如：第1次个人犯规，第3次全队犯规，全队犯规2∶3）。

- 助理记录员回复"OK"或"YES"，以确认记录屏的信息。

这样一来，记录台人员均了解了双方球队犯规和队员个人犯规的情况。这可以帮助记录台人员团队预判接下来可能发生的情况（例如：队员上半时犯规3次，或过早地达到4次犯规）。

其他职责

- 助理记录员也应当查看请求替换的队员是否有资格参加比赛。与计时员和进攻计时员就替换问题进行良好交流是非常重要的。

- 如果记录员或计时员正在忙碌，助理记录员可以喊出暂停或替换。

- 助理记录员应当负责在打架情况中观察记录台右侧的球队席区域，以确定哪些队员离开了球队席区域。

- 助理记录员应该协助计时员将全队犯规指示器放置在其一侧记录台上正确的位置。

5.4 比赛休息期间

与记录员一起，交叉检查如下重要信息：得分、犯规和暂停。

观察队员和球队席人员，在特别情况下为裁判员提供信息。

5.5 END OF GAME AND POST-GAME

Help co-officials to:

- Check that the scoreboard is accurate.
- Help the scorer to complete the scoresheet, if required.
- Sign the scoresheet.
- Observe players and bench personnel in case of any incident at the end of the game.
- Hand a copy of the scoresheet to each team.

5.5 比赛结束时和比赛结束后

协助记录台同伴完成:

- 检查记录屏的显示准确与否。
- 协助记录员完成记录表的填写（如要求的话）。
- 在记录表上签字。
- 观察队员和球队席人员，以应对比赛结束后的特别情况。
- 向双方球队分发记录表的对应联。

第 6 章
THE TIMER
计时员

THE TIMER

6.1 TIMER'S DUTIES

The timer shall:

- Measure playing time, time-outs and intervals of play.
- Ensure that the game clock signal sounds very loudly and automatically at the end of playing time in a quarter.
- Blow the whistle, simultaneously with the game clock signal sound, or use any other means possible to notify the referees immediately if the signal fails to sound or is not heard.
- Notify the teams and the referees at least 3 minutes before the third quarter is to start.
- Notify the teams and the referees when the end of time-outs or intervals of play are approaching.
- If a field goal is scored against a team which has requested a time-out, the timer shall immediately stop the game clock and sound the signal.
- Notify the referees immediately when five fouls are charged against any player.

The timer shall also:

- Indicate the number of fouls committed by each player by raising, in a manner visible to both head coaches, the marker with the number of fouls committed by that player.
- Position the team foul marker on the scorer's table, at the end nearest to the bench of the team in the team foul penalty situation, when the ball becomes live following the fourth team foul in a quarter.
- Request substitutions.
- Effect time-outs. The timer must notify the referees of the time-out opportunity when a team has requested a time-out.
- Sound the signal only when the ball becomes dead and the game clock is stopped, before the ball becomes live again. The sound of the signal does not stop the game clock or the game, nor causes the ball to become dead.

计时员

6.1 计时员的职责

计时员应当：

- 计量比赛时间、暂停时间和比赛休息期间时间。
- 确保比赛计时钟的声音信号清晰响亮，并可以在每节比赛时间结束时自动鸣响。
- 如果比赛计时钟的声音信号没有鸣响或未被听到，计时员应当同时吹响口哨，以通知裁判员。
- 在第 3 节比赛开始前至少 3 分钟时，通知双方球队和裁判员。
- 在暂停或比赛休息期间临近结束时，通知双方球队和裁判员。
- 如果非得分队请求了暂停，在对方球队得分后，计时员应当立即停止比赛计时钟并发出声音信号。
- 当任一队员出现个人 5 次犯规时，计时员应立刻通知裁判员。

计时员还应当：

- 有队员犯规时，以让双方主教练可见的方式，举起代表犯规队员的个人犯规次数的犯规指示牌。
- 当某队全队犯规在一节中累计已达 4 次且球再次成为活球时，操作放置在记录台两端最靠近双方球队席的全队犯规指示器。
- 发出替换信号。
- 发出暂停信号。当某队已提出暂停请求，在出现暂停机会时必须通知裁判员。
- 只有在球成为死球，比赛计时钟停止时，在球再次成为活球之前才能发出信号。计时员的信号不停止比赛计时钟或比赛，也不使球成为死球。

6.2 REQUIRED EQUIPMENT AND NECESSARY MATERIALS

For the game, the timer must have the following materials and equipment (supplied by the local team or organisation):

- Game clock.
- Stopwatch.
- Players foul markers.
- Team foul markers.

In addition, the following are required:

- Pens (black or blue, and red).
- Notice paper to take note of incidents (in case of a potential report to the organising body of the competition), alternating possession arrow changes and players on the court.
- A whistle or other sounding device that is different to the game clock and shot clock audible sounds.

6.3 BEFORE THE GAME

6.3.1 CHECKING THE DEVICE, SOUND AND DISPLAYS

To perform this specific task, in the presence of the referees, the timer must:

- Check that the game clock works properly (start/stop, sound signal, LEDs / display characters, lighting around the perimeter of the backboard, etc.) and is visible to the Table Officials, team benches and the spectators. The timer should also check whether the console on the table is blank or whether it shows the time in the same way as the game clock.
- Become familiar with how to use the game clock, including how to adjust the time when the clock is stopped, if this is required (in case of an error).
- Check that the stopwatch works correctly.
- Know how to set the game clock.
- Check that it is possible to see the game clock clearly at all times during the game.
- Check that the whistle-controlled time system equipment works correctly (if there is any).

6.2 所需的设备和必要的材料

比赛中，计时员必须使用以下材料和设备（主队或组织方提供）：

- 比赛计时钟。
- 秒表。
- 队员犯规指示牌。
- 全队犯规指示器。

除此之外，还应为计时员配备：

- 签字笔（黑色或蓝色和红色）。
- 记录用纸，用来记录特别情况（为完成提交赛事组织者的书面报告使用），记录交替拥有箭头变换次序，以及记录队员的上场信息。
- 一个口哨或其他声响设备，该设备的声音需要区别于比赛计时钟和进攻计时钟的声音信号。

6.3 赛前

6.3.1 检查器材、音响和显示设备

为了顺利完成这项任务，计时员必须在裁判员在场时：

- 检查比赛计时钟的运转情况（开动/停止，声音信号，LED 显示，篮板周围的灯带等），并且确保这些设备能够被记录台人员、球队席和观众所看到。记录员还要检查记录台上的比赛计时钟控制器，确认控制器上显示的时间是空白的，还是与比赛时间同步的。
- 熟练操作比赛计时钟，包括在停表时如何调整时间（如在必要时纠正失误）。
- 检查秒表是否可以正常使用。
- 知晓如何设置比赛计时钟。
- 确定是否能够在整场比赛中清晰地看到比赛计时钟。
- 确定哨声控制计时系统是否运行良好（如在比赛中使用的话）。

6.3.2   GAME CLOCK

An electronic game clock should be used to measure the playing time and the intervals, and should be located clearly visible to all those involved in the game, including the spectators.

Each duplicate game clock (if present) shall display the score and the playing time remaining throughout the game or an interval of play.

Time-outs should be timed on a separate clock to the game clock. This is to ensure that the game clock is visible to all participants and spectators during every time-out. The timer may use the stopwatch for time-outs if there is no separate visible time-out clock to do this.

6.3.3   SOUND SIGNALS

There shall be at least two separate sound signals, with distinctly different and very loud sounds:

- The first signal shall sound automatically and synchronously with the red backboard lights, to indicate the end of the playing time for a quarter.

- The second signal, independent and with a different sound to the one described above, can be activated manually, when it is appropriate to attract the attention of the referees (e.g. towards the end of intervals of play or time-outs).

- Both signals shall be sufficiently powerful to be easily heard above the most adverse or noisy conditions. The sound volume shall have the ability to be adjusted according to the size of the arena and the noise of the spectators. A connection to the public information system of the arena is strongly recommended.

- In case of time-out requests, the scorer shall only sound the signal when the ball becomes dead (game clock stopped), after the referee has ended reporting to the table (if any) and before the ball becomes live again.

6.3.2 比赛计时钟

一个电子比赛计时钟应当被用来计量比
赛时间和比赛休息期时间的，它应当位于能
够被包括观众在内的所有比赛参与者清楚观
察到的位置。

如有额外的比赛计时钟，这些比赛计时钟应在整个比赛期间或比
赛休息期间显示比分和比赛的剩余时间。

暂停时间应当在另一个单独的计时钟上显示。这是为了在暂停期
间，比赛计时钟同样能够被比赛参与者和观众看到。如果没有另一个
单独的计时钟，计时员应当使用秒表来计量暂停时间。

6.3.3 声音信号

应当至少有两个不同的声音信号，这两个信号能够被区分，并且
声音响亮：

- 第一个声音信号应自动响起、与篮板红色灯带启动同步，用以
  显示一节比赛的结束。
- 第二个独立的声音信号，声音类型应是不同于前者的。可以手
  动操作，用以吸引裁判员的注意（例如：在比赛休息期结束或
  暂停时间结束时使用）。
- 以上两个声音信号都必须是非常响亮的，应能够在相对最不利
  或最嘈杂的比赛环境中被听到。声音信号的音量应可以根据体
  育馆的大小和观众的嘈杂程度来调节。强烈推荐将声音信号系
  统接入体育馆的公共广播系统。
- 在一次请求暂停的情况下，记录员只应在球成死球（比赛计时
  钟停止），以及当裁判员已结束了与记录台的联系，并且球再
  次成为活球前发出信号。

6.3.4   PRE-GAME TIMING

The timer will start the clock 60 minutes prior to the scheduled start of the game.

7, 8 or 9 minutes (or the time indicated by the LOC) before the start of the game, the Crew Chief shall blow the whistle and ensure that all players stop their warm-up and return immediately to their respective team bench areas, at that moment the presentation of the teams begins. Following the game run-down defined by the LOC.

As an example, the chart on the right lists the elements which are mandatory for all games of the FIBA Basketball World Cup 2019 Qualifiers and shall therefore be integrated without any modifications in the sport presentation programme and Game Run-down.

If the presentation is too long, the timer will stop the clock when it shows 3:00 minutes. As soon as all the players, coaches and referees have been introduced to the spectators, the timer notifying the referees before the first and third quarter when 3 minutes remain until the quarter and the referee signals that three (3) minutes remain prior to the start of the game, using the conventional signal.

Time to tip-off	Description of activity	Music / Entertain-ment
-30:00	Official entrance of the teams and warm-up	FIBA Anthem (100")
-11:00	Teams photo session	
-09:00	Teams on team benches / Prepare for team Introductions	FIBA Anthem (60")
-08:00	Team Introductions TEAM B (VISITING)	
-07:00	Team Introductions TEAM A (HOME)	
-06:00	National Anthem TEAM B (VISITING)	
-04:45	National Anthem TEAM A (HOME)	Host country always last
-03:30	Gift Exchange	
-03:00	Final warm-up	
-01:30	Players return to bench	FIBA Anthem (6")
00:00	GAME STARTS	

The timer notifying the referees, when 1:30 minute remains until the beginning of the game, and the referee will ensure that the teams go to their team bench areas.

6.3.4 赛前的计时

计时员应在赛前 60 分钟开始计时。

在赛前 7 分钟、8 分钟或 9 分钟时（或根据当地比赛组织方的要求调整），主裁判员应鸣哨以确保双方球队停止赛前练习并立刻返回其球队席，此时应开始入场仪式。接着根据当地比赛组织方的要求进行倒计时活动。

以右表为例，此表列出了 2019 年国际篮联篮球世界杯预选赛期间所有比赛都必须具备的环节，因此，在不做任何修改的情况下，这些环节将被整合到体育展示计划和比赛活动环节中。

如果入场仪式时间太长，那么计时员可以在计时钟显示剩余 3:00 时停止计时。向观众介绍完所有队员、教练员和裁判员之后，计时员

跳球倒计时	对应的活动	音乐/娱乐节目
-30:00	球队正式入场并进行准备活动	国际篮联会歌（100秒）
-11:00	球队合照环节	
-09:00	球队各自回到球队席/做好球队介绍的准备	国际篮联会歌（60秒）
-08:00	介绍 B 队（客队）	
-07:00	介绍 A 队（主队）	
-06:00	播放 B 队国的国歌（客队）	
-04:45	播放 A 队国的国歌（主队）	主办国总是在后
-03:30	交换礼品	
-03:00	进行最后的准备活动	
-01:30	队员回到球队席	国际篮联会歌（6秒）
00:00	开始比赛	

发出声音信号，裁判员鸣哨，使用手势提醒距离第 1 节和第 3 节比赛开始剩余 3 分钟。

在距离比赛开始前剩余 1:30 时，计时员再次发出声音信号，此时裁判员应确认双方球队返回其各自球队席区域。

6.4 DURING THE GAME

6.4.1 GAME CLOCK

The game shall consist of four quarters of 10 minutes. There shall be an interval of play of 20 minutes before the game is scheduled to begin. There shall be intervals of play of 2 minutes between the first and second quarter (first half), between the third and fourth quarter (second half), and before each overtime. There shall be a half-time interval of play of 15 minutes.

INTERVAL	1st Half			HALF-TIME	2nd Half			INTERVAL	Overtimes		
	1 P	INT	2 P		3 P	INT	4 P		E.P.	INT	...
20'	10'	2'	10'	15'	10'	2'	10'	2'	5'	2'	...
	2 Time-outs				3 Time-outs				1 T-O		

An interval of play begins:
- Twenty minutes before the game is scheduled to begin.
- When the game clock signal sounds for the end of a quarter, except if the referee calls a foul at the same time as the quarter ends. In this case, the interval of play will begin when all administration connected with the foul has taken place, including any free throws.

An interval of play ends:

- At the beginning of the first quarter when the ball leaves the hand(s) of the referee on the jump ball.
- At the beginning of all other quarters when the ball is at the disposal of the player taking the throw-in at the centre line extended, opposite the scorer's table.

6.4.2 INDICATE THE NUMBER OF FOULS COMMITTED BY EACH PLAYER

The timer, while the scorer is recording a foul, shall show the foul marker reporting the number of fouls committed by that player. The timer shall follow this three-step process to ensure that the marker is visible for:

6.4 赛中

6.4.1 比赛计时钟

比赛应由 4 节组成，每节 10 分钟。在预定的比赛开始时间之前，应有 20 分钟的比赛休息期间。在第 1 节和第 2 节（上半时）之间，第 3 节和第 4 节（下半时）之间，以及每一决胜期之前，应有 2 分钟的比赛休息期间。两个半时之间的比赛休息期间应是 15 分钟。

比赛休息期间	上半时			半场比赛休息期间	下半时			比赛休息期间	决胜期		
	1 P	INT	2 P		3 P	INT	4 P		E.P.	INT	……
	10'	2'	10'		10'	2'	10'		5'	2'	……
20'	2 次暂停			15'	3 次暂停			2'	1 次暂停		

一次比赛休息期间开始于：

- 预定的比赛开始时间之前 20 分钟。
- 结束一节的比赛计时钟信号响时，除非裁判员在一节的比赛结束时宣判了一起犯规，在此情况下，比赛休息期间应在所有犯规的罚则执行完成，包括执行罚球之后，才开始。

一次比赛休息期间结束于：

- 第 1 节开始，在跳球抛球中，当球离开主裁判员的手时。
- 所有其他节的开始，当掷球入界队员在记录台对面的中线延长线可处理球时。

6.4.2 举示每名队员的犯规次数

当记录员在记录一起犯规时，计时员应举示该犯规队员对应犯规次数的犯规指示牌。计时员应依照"三步"程序以确保以下人员能够看到犯规指示牌：

1. both benches.

2. spectators, players and referees.

3. both benches (again).

The reason for showing the player foul marker towards benches twice is very simple: it is to ensure the head coach is fully aware so that a substitution can be made if required.

1   2   3

When a player reaches his/her fifth foul the timer shall sound the signal and at the same time shall show the fifth personal foul marker. In this case, it is a two-step process:

1   2

There are some special situations to consider:

a. The same player has committed more than one foul (set of fouls, in the same dead ball period);

b. Two players have committed one foul each (e.g. double foul).

1. 双方球队席。
2. 观众、队员和裁判员。
3. 双方球队席（再一次）。

向球队席举示两次犯规指示牌的理由很简单：为的是确保主教练完全清楚当前的情况并决定是否换人。

1

2

3

当任一队员达到他 / 她的第 5 次犯规时，计时员应发出信号，同时举示第 5 次个人犯规的指示牌。在此情况下，应依照"两步"程序：

1

2

需要考虑到有些特殊情况：

a. 在同一死球期间，同一名队员被宣判多起犯规。

b. 宣判两名队员的犯规（例如：双方犯规）。

Case a)

In the same hand the timer shall show the player's foul markers that correspond to the committed fouls, as shown below.

1   2   3

Case b)

In this case the timer shall take in the hand the foul marker that corresponds to the foul committed by each player. It is important to note that in the diagrams below, the Table Official is indicating that the team B player has committed his/her first foul and the team A player his/her third.

1   2   3

To be accurate, the timer must always have a hand on the operation keys of the game clock, (i.e. start/stop buttons).

【案例 a】

计时员用同一只手举起该队员的多个对应数字的犯规指示牌，如下图所示。

1

2

3

【案例 b】

在这个案例中，计时员应当用两只手分别举起犯规队员对应数字的犯规指示牌。非常重要的是，图示中记录台人员举示的犯规指示牌所示的是：B 队队员第 1 次犯规，A 队队员第 3 次犯规。

1

2

3

为了做到更加精确，计时员必须时刻置一手于操作比赛计时钟的按钮上（即开动 / 停止键）。

The timer shall measure playing time as follows:

Starting the game clock when:

- **During a jump ball**, the ball is legally tapped by a jumper.
- After an unsuccessful last or only **free throw** and the ball continues to be live, the ball touches or is touched by a player on the playing court.
- **During a throw-in**, the ball touches or is legally touched by a player on the playing court. During a throw-in, it is possible that the timer cannot see the legal touch of the ball. In this case, the timer should watch the hand signal of the referee administering the throw-in and start the clock when the referee uses the conventional signal to start the clock.

Stopping the game clock when:

- Time expires at the end of playing time for a quarter, if not stopped automatically by the game clock itself.
- A referee blows the whistle while the ball is live. In noisy games when the referee's whistle is difficult to hear, the timer should also be constantly watching for the referees using conventional signals to stop the clock.
- A field goal is scored against a team which has requested a time-out.
- A field goal is scored when the game clock shows 2:00 minutes or less in the fourth quarter and in each overtime.
- The shot clock signal sounds while a team is in control of the ball (shot clock violation), if signalled by the referees.
- A time-out is charged against the team whose coach first made a request, unless the time-out is granted following a field goal scored by the opponents and without an infraction having been called.

6.4.3   TIME-OUT AND SUBSTITUTION

Time-outs and substitutions are interruptions of the game requested respectively by the head coach and the substitute. After a request, and when an appropriate opportunity exists the scorer must notify the referee of them. To better understand the opportunities available for time-outs and substitutions we need to introduce two concepts: live ball and dead ball.

计时员应按下列所述计量比赛时间：

开动比赛计时钟，当：

- **跳球中**，球被跳球队员合法拍击时。
- 最后一次**罚球**不成功，并且球继续是活球，球接触任一场上队员或被任一场上队员接触时。
- **掷球入界中**，球接触任一场上队员或被任一场上队员合法接触时。在掷球入界中，计时员有可能无法看到球被合法接触。在这种情况下，计时员应该观察执行掷球入界的裁判员的手势，并在裁判员使用开表手势时开动计时钟。

停止比赛计时钟，当：

- 在一节比赛结束，但比赛计时钟没有自动停止时。
- 活球中裁判员鸣哨时。在嘈杂的比赛环境中，很难听到裁判员的哨声，计时员应该不断观察裁判员是否使用了停止计时钟的手势。
- 某队已请求暂停，对方队中篮得分时。
- 在第 4 节和每一决胜期比赛计时钟显示 2:00 分钟或更少时中篮得分。
- 某队控制球，进攻计时钟响起信号时（进攻时间违例），如果裁判员做出对应手势。
- 除了对方队员中篮得分并且没有发生违犯后准予的暂停外，应给首先提出暂停请求的教练员的球队登记暂停。

6.4.3 暂停和替换

暂停和替换是由主教练和替补队员各自请求的中断比赛。在发出请求后，记录员必须在合适的时机通知裁判员已经出现了暂停和替换请求。为了更好地理解暂停和替换的机会，我们需要介绍两个概念：活球和死球。

The ball becomes **live** when:

- During the jump ball, the ball leaves the hand(s) of the referee on the toss.
- During a free throw, the ball is at the disposal of the free throw shooter.
- During a throw-in, the ball is at the disposal of the player taking the throw-in.

The ball becomes **dead** when:

- Any field goal or free throw is made.
- A referee blows the whistle while the ball is live.
- It is apparent that the ball will not enter the basket on a free throw which is to be followed by:
  - Another free throw(s).
  - A further penalty (free throw(s) and/or possession).
- The game clock signal sounds for the end of the quarter.
- The shot clock signal sounds while a team is in control of the ball.
- The ball in flight on a shot for a field goal is touched by a player from either team after:
  - A referee blows the whistle.
  - The game clock signal sounds for the end of the quarter.
  - The shot clock signal sounds.

The ball does **not become dead** and the goal counts if made when:

- The ball is in flight on a shot for a field goal and:
  - A referee blows the whistle.
  - The game clock signal sounds for the end of the quarter.
  - The shot clock signal sounds.
- The ball is in flight on a free throw and a referee blows the whistle for any rule infraction other than by the free throw shooter.
- A player commits a foul on any opponent while the ball is in the control of the opponent in the act of shooting for a field goal and who finishes the shot with a continuous motion which started before the foul occurred. This provision does not apply and the goal shall not count if:
  - after a referee blows the whistle and an entirely new act of shooting is made.
  - during the continuous motion of a player in the act of shooting the game clock signal sounds for an end of quarter or the shot clock signal sounds.

球成**活球**，当：
- 跳球中，球离开主裁判员抛球的手时。
- 罚球中，罚球队员可处理球时。
- 掷球入界中，掷球入界队员可处理球时。

球成**死球**，当：
- 任何中篮或罚球中篮时。
- 活球中，裁判员鸣哨时。
- 在一次罚球中球明显不会进入球篮，且该次罚球后接着有：
  - 另外的罚球时。
  - 进一步的罚则（罚球和／或掷球入界）时。
- 比赛计时钟信号响以结束一节比赛时。
- 某队控制球，进攻计时钟信号响时。
- 投篮中飞行的球在下述情况后被任一队的队员接触时：
  - 裁判员鸣哨。
  - 比赛计时钟信号响以结束一节比赛。
  - 进攻计时钟信号响。

球**不成死球**，如中篮计得分，当：
- 投篮的球在飞行中，并且：
  - 裁判员鸣哨。
  - 比赛计时钟信号响以结束一节比赛。
  - 进攻计时钟信号响。
- 罚球的球在飞行中，并且裁判员因除罚球队员之外的任何人员违犯规则而鸣哨。
- 一名投篮队员控制着球时，对方队任何队员或允许坐在对方队球队席的任何人员被犯规，该投篮队员以连续动作完成了犯规发生前已开始的投篮。 如果：
  - 在裁判员鸣哨后做了一个全新的投篮动作。
  - 该投篮队员在做连续动作期间比赛计时钟信号响以结束一节或进攻计时钟信号响。

6.4.3.1 TIME-OUT REQUEST

As stated above a time-out is an interruption of the game requested by the head coach or first assistant coach. Each time-out shall last one minute.

A time-out opportunity begins when:

- For both teams, the ball becomes dead, the game clock is stopped and the referee has ended the signalling (in case of violations) and / or communication with the Table Officials (in case of foul).

- For both teams, the ball becomes dead following a successful last or only free throw.

- For the non-scoring team, a field goal is scored.

- **In any case that IRS is used, for both teams after the final IRS decision.**

A time-out opportunity ends when the ball is at the disposal of a player for a throw-in or for a first or only free throw (live ball).

- A time-out cannot be granted before the playing time for a quarter has started or after the playing time for a quarter has ended.

The ball is at the disposal of a player for a first or only free throw.

The ball is at the disposal of a player for a throw-in.

- If the request for the time-out is made by either team after the ball is at the disposal of the free throw shooter for the first or only free throw, the time-out shall be granted if:

  1. The last or only free throw is successful.

  2. The last or only free throw is followed by a throw-in from the throw-in line at the team's front court.

6.4.3.1 暂停请求

如上所述，主教练或第一助理教练请求中断比赛是暂停。每次暂停应持续 1 分钟。

一次暂停机会开始，当：

- 对于双方队，球成死球，比赛计时钟停止，以及当裁判员已完成了手势（如有违规）和/或结束了与记录台的联系时（如有犯规）。
- 对于双方队，在最后一次罚球成功后，球成死球时。

- 对于非得分队，中篮得分时。
- **对于双方队，在即时回放复审结束后，并且在裁判员报告最终决定后。**

当队员在掷球入界或第一次或唯一一次罚球（活球）可处理球时，**一次暂停机会结束。**

- 在任一节比赛开始前或任一节比赛结束后，不能准予暂停。

第一次或仅有一次的罚球中，罚球队员可处理球时。

掷球入界中，掷球入界队员可处理球时。

- 如果第一次或仅有一次的罚球，球置于罚球队员可处理之后，任一队请求了一次暂停，则在下列情况下暂停应被准予：

1. 最后一次或仅有一次的罚球成功。

2. 最后一次或仅有一次的罚球后，在该队前场的掷球入界线执行掷球入界。

3. A foul is called between free throws. In this case the throw(s) shall be completed and the time-out shall be permitted before the new foul penalty is administered, unless otherwise stated in the OBR.

4. A foul is called before the ball becomes live after the last free throw. In this case the time-out shall be permitted before the new foul penalty is administered.

5. A violation is called before the ball becomes live after the last free throw. In this case the time-out shall be permitted before the throw-in is administered.

- In the event of consecutive sets of free throws and/or possession of the ball resulting from more than one foul penalty, each set is to be treated separately.

- A time-out shall not be permitted to the scoring team when the game clock shows 2:00 minutes or less in the fourth quarter and in each overtime and, following a successful field goal unless a referee has interrupted the game.

- When the game clock shows 2:00 minutes or less in the fourth quarter and in each overtime, following a time-out taken by the team that is entitled to possession of the ball from its backcourt, the head coach of that team has the right to decide whether the game shall be resumed with a throw-in from the throw-in line at the team's frontcourt or from the team's backcourt at the place nearest to where the game was stopped.

If a time-out opportunity has just ended and a coach runs to the scorer's table, loudly requesting a time-out and the timer reacts and erroneously sounds the signal, the referee blows the whistle and interrupts the game, the game shall resume immediately. The request was made too late and, the time-out shall not be granted.

A time-out is charged against the team whose coach first made a request unless the time-out is granted following a field goal scored by the opponents and without an infraction having been called. In this case, it is necessary to notify the coaches who the time-out was charged to, and to ask the coach if the pending time-out request is still valid. This is important, especially in the last 2 minutes of the game.

Procedure

After a time-out request, during the time-out opportunity the timer shall notify the referees by sounding the signal and giving the time-out signal (see below). It is a two-step signalling process: the timer gives the time-out signal and then indicates the bench of the team who requested the time-out, showing an open palm for higher visibility.

3. 在多次罚球之间发生了犯规。这种情况下，应完成该罚球单元，在新的犯规罚则执行之前允许暂停，除非本规则另有规定。

4. 在最后一次罚球后，在球成活球前发生了一次犯规。这种情况下，在执行新的犯规罚则之前允许暂停。

5. 在最后一次罚球后，在球成活球前发生了一次违例。这种情况下，在执行掷球入界之前允许暂停。

- 如果一个以上的犯规罚则造成连续的罚球单元和／或球权，每个单元分别处理。
- 在第 4 节和每一决胜期的比赛计时钟显示 2:00 分钟或更少时，在一次中篮成功后，不允许得分队暂停，除非裁判员已中断了比赛。
- 当第 4 节和每一决胜期中的比赛计时钟显示 2:00 分钟或更少时，已判给在后场拥有球权的队被准予了暂停，暂停结束后，该队主教练有权决定是在其前场的掷球入界线还是在后场最靠近比赛停止的地点掷球入界。

如果一次暂停机会刚刚结束，教练员跑到记录台大声请求暂停，并且计时员错误地做出反应发出了声音信号，随后裁判员鸣哨打断比赛，此时比赛应当立即重新开始。该暂停请求得太迟，所以不应被准予。

除了对方队员中篮得分并且没有发生违犯后准予的暂停外，应给首先提出暂停请求的主教练或第一助理教练的球队登记暂停。在此情况下，有必要通知被准予暂停的教练员，并询问另一名教练员是否还需请求未执行的暂停。这样的操作规范，在比赛的最后 2 分钟格外重要。

程序

球队请求暂停后，暂停机会一开始，计时员就应发出信号并通过手势通知裁判员已有球队提出了暂停请求（见下图）。该程序有 2 个步骤：计时员做出暂停手势，然后指出请求暂停的球队，应打开手掌做手势以获得更高的可见度。

When the referee confirms the time-out, the scorer should record it on the scoresheet as described earlier.

The coach requests a time-out	
The timer sounds the signal and makes the time-out signal, when there is an opportunity	
The referee blows the whistle and makes the signal. The time-out begins	
The players stay in the bench area	
The timer sounds the signal when 50" and 1 minute of the time-out have elapsed	

当裁判员确认了暂停，记录员应如之前所述，在记录表上记录暂停信息。

教练员请求一次暂停	
当出现一次暂停机会时，计时员发出信号并做出暂停手势	 
裁判员鸣哨并做出暂停手势。暂停时段开始	
队员们停留在其球队席区域	
计时员在暂停时间走过 50 秒和 1 分钟时发出信号	

- Only a head coach or first assistant coach has the right to request a time-out. They shall establish visual contact with the scorer or go to the scorer's table and ask clearly for a time-out, making the proper conventional sign with their hands. To gain visibility, the coach can approach the table. The timer must call the time-out at the first opportunity.

- Conditional requests are not allowed. For example, it is not permitted for a coach to say "Time-out if they score".

- A time-out request may be cancelled only before the timer's signal has sounded for such a request.

- The time-out period begins when a referee blows the whistle and gives the time-out signal. It ends when a referee blows the whistle and beckons the teams back on to the playing court. If, following a request for a time-out, a foul is committed by either team, the time-out shall not begin until the referee has completed all communication related to that foul with the scorer's table. In the case of a fifth foul by a player, this communication includes the necessary substitution procedure. Once completed, the time-out period shall begin when a referee blows the whistle and gives the time-out signal. Teams shall be permitted to go to their benches if they are aware that a time-out has been requested, even though the time-out period has not formally begun.

- As soon as a time-out opportunity begins, the timer shall sound the signal to notify the referees that a request for a time-out has been made. If a field goal is scored against a team which has requested a time-out, the timer shall immediately stop the game clock and sound the signal.

- 只有主教练或第一助理教练有权请求暂停。他们应与记录台建立目光沟通或到记录台处清楚地要求暂停，并用手做出正确的常规手势。为了让记录台更容易注意到暂停请求，教练员可以靠近记录台提出请求。计时员必须在出现第一次暂停机会时发出信号。

- 条件性的请求是不被允许的。比如：教练员提出"如果他们得分我们就要暂停"是不被允许的。

- 一次暂停请求只可在计时员发出该次暂停请求的信号之前被取消。

- 当裁判员鸣哨并给出暂停手势时，暂停时段开始。当裁判员鸣哨并招呼球队回到比赛场地上时，暂停时段结束。如果一队请求暂停后，任  一球队犯规了，应等到裁判员完成与记录台的一切沟通后才开始暂停时段。在出现队员 5 次犯规的情况下，该沟通还应包括必要的替换程序。在完成这些程序后，裁判员鸣哨并给出暂停手势，此时暂停时段开始。当球队意识到他们已经请求了暂停后，即使暂停时段没有正式开始，应允许双方队员回到他们的球队席。

- 当一次暂停机会出现，计时员应当发出声音信号通知裁判员有球队请求了暂停。非得分队请求暂停后，如果中篮了，计时员应当立即停表，并发出声音信号。

SUMMARY	GAME CLOCK	STATUS OF THE BALL	TIME-OUT ALLOWED
PLAYING	Running	Live	NO
REFEREE BLOWS THE WHISTLE	Stopped	Dead	BOTH TEAMS
DEAD BALL			
BALL AT DISPOSAL		Live	NO

Procedure

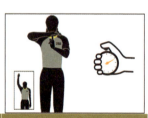

The coach requests a time-out	The timer sounds his/her signal and makes the time-out signal when there is an opportunity	The referee blows the whistle and makes the signal. The time-out begins and the timer starts the stopwatch

综述	比赛计时钟	球的状态	是否允许暂停
比赛进行中	运行期间	活球	不允许
裁判员鸣哨	停止期间	死球	允许给予双方队
死球			
可处理球		活球	不允许

程序：

教练员请求一次暂停	当出现一次暂停机会时，计时员发出信号并做出暂停手势	裁判员鸣哨并做出暂停手势。暂停时段开始，计时员启动秒表

The players stay in the team bench area	The timer sounds his/her signal when 50" and 1 minute of the time-out have passed.

The timer shall measure a time-out as follows:

- Starting the stopwatch immediately when the referee blows the whistle and gives the time-out signal.
- Sounding the signal when 50 seconds of the time-out have elapsed and showing the appropriate signal that ten (10) seconds are left to the end of the time-out.
- Sounding the signal when the time-out has ended.

If during the time-out, a substitution has been requested, the timer shall make the conventional substitution signal when sounding the horn (10 sec. left on the clock). After making the conventional substitution signal, the timer shall also indicate the team or teams who have requested the substitution.

- In case of failure of the device, the timer shall (if the game clock does not start):
  - Start the stopwatch timer (usually used to measure time-outs).
  - Advise the Commissioner, if present.
  - If not, stand up to be more visible (so that the referees can note that there is a problem).
  - When the ball becomes dead, stop the watch and inform the referee that the game clock was stopped(e.g. for 5 seconds).

When the assistant scorer is not present, it is the timer who updates the scoreboard. During play, starting and stopping the game clock correctly is more important than updating the scoreboard. For this reason, during the game the timer must be aware for time-out request when a field goal is scored and, especially in the last 2 minutes of the game, the timer must stop the game clock when a field goal is scored, and only when the game clock has been started (according to the rule) the score on the scoreboard can be updated.

| 队员们停留在其球队席区域 | 计时员在暂停时间走过第 50 秒时和 1 分钟时发出信号 |

计时员应按下列所述计量暂停:

- 裁判员鸣哨并给出暂停手势,立即开动秒表。
- 当暂停已过去 50 秒时发出信号,并在还有 10 秒时做出合适的手势。
- 当暂停已结束时发出信号。

如果,在一起暂停期间又出现了替换请求,计时员应在暂停时段还剩 10 秒时发出信号并做出替换手势。在计时员做出替换手势后,计时员还应指出请求替换的球队。

- 在计时设备失效的情况下(如果比赛计时钟没有开动),计时员还应当:
  - 开动秒表来计量时间(通常用来计量暂停时段)。
  - 告知到场的技术代表。
  - 如果计时钟没有开动,应站起来吸引大家的注意(让裁判员意识到出现了问题)。
  - 当球成死球时,停止计时的秒表,并告知裁判员比赛计时钟已被停止(例如:停止了 5 秒)。

如果没有助理记录员,那么计时员应当操作记录屏。比赛过程中,正确地开表和停表,比更新记录屏更为重要。基于此,计时员必须时刻留意中篮得分后是否有球队请求暂停,尤其是在比赛的最后 2 分钟,计时员必须在球中篮后依照规则停止和开动比赛计时钟,只有在开动了比赛计时钟后,才操作记录屏。

Simultaneously with the end of the quarter, the timer must blow the whistle if the game clock's signal / sound fails, or the referees cannot hear it, so that the referees can be notified of the end of the quarter.

Helping partners during the game

- Repeat periodically and loudly how long is left on the clock, so that the whole Table Officials crew know the time left to play, even in the case of a game clock failure. This should be agreed to in the pre-game meeting among the Table Officials crew.

- Count down loudly the final 5 seconds of each 24-second offence - once the shot clock operator has called out "ten seconds", meaning there are ten seconds remaining on the shot clock.

- When the whistle-controlled time system is used, sometimes the timing devices on the referees' belt does not work correctly (due to Wi-Fi interferences). The timer shall constantly verify if the whistle-controlled time system device is working correctly and notify the referees if it is not.

- Call loudly to the scorer if substitutions or time-outs are requested from the bench to the left of the scorer's table and notify new entries to the scorer.

- Observe the playing court and note down details of any incidents in case of fighting and bench clearances.

6.4.3.2   SUBSTITUTION REQUESTS

A substitution is an interruption of the game requested by the substitute to become a player. A team may substitute more than one player during a substitution opportunity.

Substitutions cannot be granted before the game has begun (except in the case of an injury to a starting five player during the warm up).

如果在一节比赛结束时比赛计时钟信号 / 声音未响，计时员必须在此时鸣哨，否则裁判员无法得知该节已结束。计时员鸣哨就是为了通知裁判员该节已结束。

比赛中协助同伴

- 不间断和大声地重复说出比赛计时钟的剩余时间，这可以使记录台人员清楚地知道比赛的剩余时间，即便在比赛计时钟失效的情况下也应如此。该程序应在记录台人员的赛前准备会中达成共识。

- 大声倒计时进攻计时钟的最后 5 秒。一旦进攻计时员说出"10秒"，这意味着进攻计时钟还剩 10 秒。

- 在使用哨声控制计时系统的比赛中，裁判员腰带上的操作设备有时可能会因为 Wi-Fi 设备的原因而不能正常工作。计时员需要持续关注这套设备是否工作正常，如未正常工作，则必须通知裁判员。

- 如在记录台左侧有相关人员请求替换或暂停，计时员应大声告知记录员，并将新上场的队员告知记录员。

- 在打架时，观察比赛场上和球队席的情况，并且记录这些特别情况的所有细节。

6.4.3.2 替换请求

替补队员请求中断比赛成为队员是一次替换。在一次替换机会期间球队可以替换多名队员。

比赛开始前，不得准予替换（除非 5 名首发队员中的一名在赛前热身期间受伤）。

A substitution opportunity begins when:

- For both teams, the ball becomes dead, the game clock is stopped and the referee has ended the communication with the scorer's table.

- For both teams, the ball becomes dead following a successful last or only free throw.

- For the non-scoring team, a field goal is scored when the game clock shows 2:00 minutes or less in the fourth quarter and in each overtime.

A substitution opportunity ends when:

The ball is at the disposal of a player for a first or only free throw

The ball is at the disposal of a player for a throw-in

Players who have been designated by the coach to start the game may be substituted in the event of an injury. In this case, the opponents are also entitled to substitute the same number of players, if they so wish.

Similarly on free throws, if the referee notices after the first free throw that the shooter is bleeding, the player must be substituted and the opponents may also make a substitution if they so wish.

If a substitution opportunity has just ended and a player runs to the scorer's table, loudly requesting a substitution and the scorer reacts and erroneously sounds the signal, the referee blows the whistle and interrupts the game, the game shall resume immediately. The request was made too late and the substitution shall not be granted.

一次替换机会开始，当：

- 对于双方队，当球成死球，比赛计时钟停止，以及裁判员已结束了与记录台的沟通时。

- 对于双方队，在最后一次罚球成功后，球成为死球时。
- 对于非得分队，在第 4 节和每一决胜期的比赛计时钟显示 2:00 分钟或更少，中篮得分时。

一次替换机会结束于，当：

第一次或仅有一次的
罚球的队员可处理球时

掷球入界的队员可处理球时

因为受伤，已经被主教练指定为比赛开始时上场的队员可以被替换。在此情况下，如果对方也希望替换，他们有权替换相同数量的队员。

同样，在罚球期间，如果裁判员在第一次罚球后注意到罚球队员正在流血，该罚球队员必须被替换。在此情况下，如果对方也希望替换，他们有权替换队员。

如果一次替换机会刚刚结束，替补队员跑到记录台大声请求暂停，并且计时员错误地做出反应发出了声音信号，随后裁判员鸣哨打断比赛，此时比赛应当立即重新开始。该替换请求得太迟，所以不应被准予。

A player who has become a substitute and a substitute who has become a player cannot respectively re-enter the game or leave the game until the ball becomes dead again, after a clock-running phase of the game, unless:

- The team is reduced to fewer than five players on the playing court.

- The player entitled to the free throws as the result of the correction of an error is on the team bench after having been legally substituted.

Procedure

- Only a substitute has the right to request a substitution. The substitute (not the head coach or first assistant coach) shall go to the scorer's table and ask clearly for a substitution, making the proper conventional signal with hands, or sit on the substitution chair. The substitute must be ready to play immediately.

- A substitution request may be cancelled only before the timer's signal has sounded for such a request.

- As soon as a substitution opportunity begins, the timer shall sound the signal to notify the referees that a request for a substitution has been made using the following signals:

  1. The conventional signal for a substitution.
  2. Points in the direction of the team bench requesting the substitution.

队员已成为替补队员和替补队员已成为队员，分别不能重新进入比赛或离开比赛，直到一个比赛的计时钟运行片段之后球再次成死球为止。除非：

- 某队能够上场的队员少于5名。
- 作为纠正失误的结果，拥有罚球权的队员已被合法地替换后坐在球队席上。

程序

- 只有替补队员有权请求替换。替补队员（不是主教练或第一助理教练）应到记录台清楚地要求替换，用双手做出常规替换手势或者坐在替换的椅子上。替补队员必须立即做好比赛的准备。
- 一次替换请求可以被取消，但只可在计时员发出该次替换请求的信号之前。
- 替换机会一开始，计时员就应发出信号通知裁判员替换请求已提出，并做出如下手势：
1. 做出替换的常规手势。
2. 指向请求替换队的球队席方向。

If players from both teams have requested substitutions, then the timer shall indicate this as shown below.

- The substitute shall remain outside the boundary line until the referee blows the whistle, gives the substitution signal and beckons the substitute to enter the playing court.

The player being substituted is permitted to go directly to the team bench without reporting to the officials.

- Substitutions shall be completed as quickly as possible. A player who has committed five fouls or has been disqualified must be substituted immediately (within approximately 30 seconds, timed by the timer on a manual stopwatch if necessary).

- If a substitution is requested during a time-out or an interval of play, the timer must notify the referee by giving the signal below when the time indicates that only 10 seconds are left to the end of the time-out, or that 30 seconds are left of the interval. As shown before, the timer must also indicate the team who requested the substitution.

如果双方队员请求替换，计时员应当按下图所示做出手势。

- 替补队员应停留在界线外，直到
  裁判员鸣哨，给出替换手势和招
  呼替补队员进入比赛场地。

已被替换的队员不必向裁判员或计
时员报告，被允许直接去他/她的球队席。

- 替换应尽可能快地完成。已发生第 5 次犯规或已被取消比赛资
  格的队员必须立即被替换（不超过 30 秒，如有必要的话由计
  时员使用手工秒表计时）。
- 如果在一次暂停或比赛休息期间请求替换，计时员应在暂停时
  段还剩 10 秒或比赛休息期间还剩 30 秒时发出信号并做出下图
  的手势。如之前所示，计时员还必须指出请求替换的球队。

- If the request for a substitution is made by either team after the ball is at the disposal of the free throw shooter for the first or only free throw, the substitution shall be granted if:
  - The last or only free throw is successful.
  - The last or only free throw, if not successful, is followed by a throw-in from the throw-in line at the team's frontcourt.
  - A foul is called between free throws. In this case the free throws will be completed and the substitution will be permitted before the new foul penalty is administered.
  - A foul is called before the ball becomes live after the last free throw. In this case the substitution shall be permitted before the new foul penalty is administered.
  - A violation is called before the ball becomes live after the last free throw. In this case the substitution shall be permitted before the throw-in is administered.

  In the event of consecutive sets of free throws resulting from more than 1 foul penalty, each set is to be treated separately.

- If the free throw shooter must be substituted because he/she:
  - Is injured.
  - Has committed five (5) fouls.
  - Has been disqualified.

    The free throw(s) must be attempted by the substitute who may not be substituted again until the next clock-running phase of the game has been played.

- A substitute becomes a player and a player becomes a substitute when:
  - The referee beckons the substitute to enter the playing court.
  - During a time-out or an interval of play, a substitute requests the substitution to the timer.

- A substitution request may be cancelled only before the timer's signal has sounded for such a request.

- When a player commits his/her fourth foul, the Table Officials should anticipate a possible substitution and be alert to last-minute requests.

- 第一次或仅有一次的罚球，球置于罚球队员可处理球之后，如果任一队请求替换，则在下列情况下替换应被准予：
  - 最后一次或仅有一次的罚球成功。
  - 如果最后一次或仅有一次的罚球不成功，随后须在该队前场的掷球入界线执行掷球入界。
  - 在多次罚球之间发生了犯规。这种情况下，多次罚球应完成，在新的犯规罚则执行之前允许替换。
  - 在最后一次的罚球后，在球成活球前发生了一次犯规。这种情况下，在执行新的犯规罚则之前应允许替换。
  - 在最后一次的罚球后，在球成活球前发生了一次违例。这种情况下，在执行掷球入界之前应允许替换。

如果一个以上的犯规罚则带来连续的罚球单元和／或球权，每个单元分别处理。

- 如果罚球队员：
  - 受伤。
  - 已发生第5次犯规。
  - 已被取消比赛资格。

他／她必须被替换。罚球必须由替换他／她的替补队员执行，并且该替补队员在比赛的下一个计时钟运行片段前，不能再次被替换。

- 一名替补队员成为队员和一名队员成为替补队员：
  - 当裁判员招呼替补队员进入比赛场地时。
  - 在暂停或比赛休息期间，一名替补队员向计时员请求替换时。
- 一次替换请求可以被取消，但只可在计时员发出该次替换请求的信号之前。
- 当一名队员积累到了他／她的5次个人犯规时，记录台人员应预判到可能出现的替换，并时刻留意最后时刻会出现的请求。

A substitution request can be called for both teams only when the 3 following conditions occur:

- Dead ball.
- Game clock stopped.
- The referee has ended signalling.

When the game clock shows 2.00 minutes or less in the fourth quarter and in each overtime, the Table Officials can call a substitution opportunity for the non-scoring team (called by the Timer) when 2 conditions occur:

- Dead ball.
- Game clock stopped.

In case of a substitution request and time-out request, it is very important to respect the order of the requests:

- First a substitution and after the time-out, or
- First a time-out and after the substitution.

SUMMARY	GAME CLOCK	STATUS OF THE BALL	SUBSTITUTION OPPORTUNITY
DURING THE GAME (EXCEPT 2:00 OR LESS IN THE 4TH QUARTER AND OVERTIME)			
PLAYING	Running	Live	NO
GOAL IS MADE	Running	Dead	NO
DEAD BALL	Running	Dead	NO
BALL IS AT THE DISPOSAL OF A PLAYER FOR THE THROW-IN	Running	Live	NO

在下列三种情况下，双方队均可以请求一次替换：

- 死球。
- 比赛计时钟停止。
- 裁判员已完成其手势。

当第 4 节和每一决胜期比赛计时钟显示 2:00 分钟或更少时，记录台人员可以在下列两种情况下给予非得分队替换的机会：

- 死球。
- 比赛计时钟停止。

在出现同时请求替换和暂停的情况下，遵照请求提出的顺序很重要：

- 首先是替换，然后是暂停，或
- 首先是暂停，然后是替换。

综述	比赛计时钟	球的状态	替换机会
在比赛期间（除第 4 节和决胜期比赛计时钟显示 2:00 分钟或更少时）			
比赛进行中	运行期间	活球	未出现
球中篮		死球	未出现
死球			未出现
掷球入界队员可处理球		活球	未出现

SUMMARY	GAME CLOCK	STATUS OF THE BALL	SUBSTITUTION OPPORTUNITY
THE GAME CLOCK SHOWS 2:00 MINUTES OR LESS IN THE 4TH QUARTER AND OVERTIME			
PLAYING WITH 2:00 TO GO IN LAST QUARTER OR OVERTIME	Running	Live	NO
GOAL IS MADE	Stopped	Dead	FOR THE NON-SCORING TEAM
DEAD BALL	Stopped	Dead	FOR THE NON-SCORING TEAM
BALL IS AT THE DISPOSAL OF A PLAYER FOR THE THROW-IN	Stopped	Live	NO

SUMMARY	GAME CLOCK	STATUS OF THE BALL	SUBSTITUTION OPPORTUNITY
DURING FREE THROWS			
PLAYER IS SHOOTING THE FREE THROW	Stopped	Live	NO
LAST FREE-THROW IS SCORED	Stopped	Dead	FOR BOTH TEAMS
THE BALL REMAINS DEAD	Stopped	Dead	FOR BOTH TEAMS
BALL IS AT THE DISPOSAL OF A PLAYER FOR THE THROW-IN	Stopped	Live	NO

综述	比赛计时钟	球的状态	替换机会
在第 4 节和决胜期比赛计时钟显示 2:00 分钟或更少时			
最后一节或决胜期中，比赛剩余 2:00	运行期间	活球	未出现
球中篮	停止期间	死球	准予非得分队
死球			
掷球入界队员可处理球		活球	未出现

综述	比赛计时钟	球的状态	替换机会
在罚球期间			
队员正在执行罚球	停止期间	活球	未出现
最后一次罚球中篮得分		死球	准予双方队
球仍是死球状态			
掷球入界队员可处理球		活球	未出现

191

If the referees discover that more than five players of the same team are participating on the playing court simultaneously, the error must be corrected as soon as possible without placing the opponents at a disadvantage.

Assuming that the referees and the Table Officials are doing their job correctly, one player must have re-entered or remained on the playing court illegally. The referees must therefore order one player to leave the playing court immediately and charge a technical foul against the coach of that team, recorded as 'B'. The coach is responsible for ensuring that a substitution is applied correctly and that the substituted player leaves the playing court immediately after the substitution.

6.4.4   INTERVALS OF PLAY

The timer shall take the following steps during intervals of play:

- Ensure the pre-game countdown is running when there are 20 minutes left to start the game.
- Ensure the referees are on the court in time to start quarter 1 and quarter 3. If necessary the commissioner, if present, should go to the referees' locker room to remind them.
- In the intervals between quarters 1 and 2 and between quarters 3 and 4 will start the timer with 2 minutes.
- Observe players and team bench personnel and inform the referees if there are any incidents during intervals of play.
- The timer notifying the referees before quarters 1 and 3 when three minutes, and one minute and thirty seconds remain until the beginning of the quarter.
- The timer notifying the referees 30 seconds before quarters 2 and 4 (and each overtime).
- Start the countdown of the interval of play, when the referees have indicated that a quarter of play has ended.
- At the end of the interval reset the visible game clock ready to begin a new quarter of 10 minutes, (or 5 minutes for overtimes).
- Sound the signal and simultaneously reset the game clock immediately when an interval of play has ended.

如果裁判员发现同一队同时有 5 名以上的队员在赛场上比赛，只要不置对方于不利，该失误必须立即予以纠正。

　　假定裁判员和记录台人员正在正确地工作，必定有一名队员非法进入或留在了赛场上。因此裁判员必须要求该队员立即离开赛场并应登记该队主教练一起技术犯规，记录为"B"。确保每一次替换被正确实施是主教练的责任，并且被替换的队员在替换后应立即离开赛场。

6.4.4 比赛休息期间

计时员在比赛休息期间应当遵循如下步骤：

- 距离比赛开始 20 分钟时，确认赛前的计时钟倒计时正常运行。
- 确认第 1 节、第 3 节开始前，裁判员及时出现在比赛场地。如有必要，到场的技术代表应当去更衣室提醒他们。
- 在第 1 节和第 2 节之间，以及第 3 节和第 4 节之间的比赛休息期间，开动 2 分钟的倒计时。
- 观察队员和球队席人员，如果在比赛休息期间发生特别情况，应通知裁判员。
- 第 1 节、第 3 节的赛前 3 分钟、1 分 30 秒时，发出信号通知裁判员距离比赛开始的剩余时间。
- 第 2 节、第 4 节（和每一决胜期）的赛前 30 秒时，发出信号通知裁判员距离比赛开始的剩余时间。
- 当裁判员鸣哨结束一节比赛时，开启比赛休息期间的倒计时。
- 比赛休息期间结束时，复位可见的比赛计时钟至新的一节比赛的 10 分钟（或决胜期的 5 分钟）。
- 比赛休息期间结束时，记录员应当发出信号，并且立即复位计时钟。

6.5 AFTER THE GAME

- Help the scorer to complete the scoresheet, if required.
- Sign the scoresheet.

6.5 赛后

- 如需要，协助记录员完成记录表的填写。
- 在记录表上签名。

第 7 章

THE SHOT CLOCK OPERATOR

进攻计时员

THE SHOT CLOCK OPERATOR

7.1 SHOT CLOCK OPERATOR'S DUTIES

Whenever a team gains control of a live ball on the playing court, that team must attempt a shot for a field goal within 24 seconds. The main duty of the shot clock operator is to measure this time.

7.2 REQUIRED EQUIPMENT AND NECESSARY MATERIAL

For the game, the shot clock operator must have the following equipment.

From the local team or organization:

- Shot clock device.

In addition, the following items are required:

- Pens.
- Notice paper to take note of any incidents (that can then be used to make a possible report to the organising body of the competition), alternating possession arrow changes, players on the court and so on.
- A stopwatch.
- A whistle.

7.3 BEFORE THE GAME

7.3.1 THE SHOT CLOCK DEVICE

There are several models of shot clock devices and each of them has different mechanical operations.

In general, the device should:

- Have a start / stop button or lever.
- Have two separate buttons / levers for 24 and 14 seconds reset.

进攻计时员

7.1 进攻计时员的职责

　　某队在场上控制活球时，该队必须在 24 秒内尝试投篮。进攻计时员的主要职责是计量该时段。

7.2 所需的设备和必要的材料

　　为了比赛顺利进行，进攻计时员必须有如下设备。

　　主队或组织方应提供：

- 进攻计时钟设备。

　　除此之外，还应为进攻计时员配备：

- 笔。
- 记录用纸，用来记录特别情况（为完成提交赛事组织者的书面报告使用），记录交替拥有箭头变换次序，以及记录队员的上场信息。
- 秒表。
- 口哨。

7.3 赛前

7.3.1 进攻计时钟设备

　　目前，市面上有很多种进攻计时钟设备，而且每一种都有不同的操作方法。

　　通常来说，进攻计时钟设备应当：

- 有开动和停止的按钮或操纵杆。
- 有两个独立的按钮或操纵杆来复位至 24 秒和 14 秒。

- Show the countdown in seconds.
- Not show any digits (be blank) when no team has control of the ball or when there are less than 24 / 14 seconds left to play in each quarter or overtime (the blanked position should be tied to the reset buttons).
- Reset to either 24 or 14 seconds whenever this is required.
- The sound signal should be stopped when a new period of 24 / 14 is assigned.

For Levels 1 and 2 Competitions, the shot clock display unit, together with a duplicate game clock and a red light shall:

- Be mounted on each backboard support structure or hung from the ceiling.
- Have different colours for the numbers of the shot clock and the duplicate game clock displays.
- Show the countdown in seconds and the last 5 seconds of the action in tenths (1/10) as well.

For Level 1, there must be (3) or (4) display surfaces per unit (recommended for Levels 2 and 3) which must be clearly visible to everyone involved in the game, including the spectators.

7.3.2 CHECKING THE DEVICE, SIGNAL SOUND AND DISPLAY

Both the shot clock operator and timer are responsible for handling the electronic devices. The high performance of these devices is essential to enable each of these Table Officials to carry out their roles to the highest standard.

In general, the device should:

- Have a separate control unit provided for the shot clock operator, with a very loud automatic signal to indicate the end of the shot clock period when the display shows zero (0).
- Have a display unit with a digital countdown, indicating the time in seconds only.
- Start from 24/14 seconds.
- Be stopped with the display indicating the time remaining.
- Be restarted from the time at which it was stopped.
- Show no display, if necessary.

For levels 1 and 2 the shot clock display unit , together with a duplicate game clock shall:

- Have the signal sounding for the end of the shot clock period when the display shows zero (0.0).

- 具备倒计时显示功能。
- 在没有球队控制球或距离每一节或决胜期结束少于 24 秒或 14 秒时，可以清屏（清屏按钮应与复位键绑定在一起）。
- 随时可以根据规则复位至 24 秒或 14 秒。
- 当复位至一个新的 24 秒或 14 秒周期后，声音信号应停止。

在国际篮联的一级和二级比赛中，进攻计时钟设备，连同额外的比赛计时钟和红色灯光设备应：

- 安装在每个篮板后方篮架的支撑物上或悬吊在天花板上。
- 进攻计时钟上显示进攻时间数字的颜色和同步比赛计时钟数字的颜色应不同。
- 以整秒显示倒计时，并在最后 5 秒时以 1/10 秒显示。

在国际篮联的一级比赛中，进攻计时钟设备必须有 3 个或 4 个显示面（同样推荐二级和三级比赛使用），该显示方式必须使包括观众在内的所有比赛参与者能够清晰地看到时间信息。

7.3.2 检查进攻计时钟设备、声音信号和显示

进攻计时员和计时员负责操作电子设备。这些电子计时设备从本质上必须具备能够承载这两位记录台人员高标准工作表现的良好性能。

通常来说，进攻计时钟设备应当：

- 为进攻计时员备有一个独立的控制器，并可以在进攻计时周期结束显示零秒（0.0）时，自动发出非常响亮的声音信号。
- 具备电子倒计时功能，仅显示秒数。
- 可以从 24 秒或 14 秒开始倒计时。
- 在停止时，显示剩余时间。
- 可以从停止的时间重新开始。
- 在需要时，不显示进攻时间。

在国际篮联的一级和二级比赛中，进攻计时钟设备，连同额外的比赛计时钟应：

- 在进攻计时周期结束显示零秒（0.0）时，发出声音信号。

- Indicate the time remaining in seconds; and tenths (1/10) of a second only during the last 5 seconds of the shot clock period.

- Be mounted on each backboard support structure a minimum or hung from the ceiling.

- Have the numbers of the shot clock in red colour and the numbers of the duplicate game clock in yellow colour.

- Have the numbers of the shot clock display a minimum height of 230 mm and be larger than the numbers of the duplicate game clock.

- Have electromagnetic compatibility in accordance with the statutory requirements of the respective country.

The fact that there are different types of consoles means that it is very important to take time before starting the game (during the check of devices and during the pre-game interval), to become familiar with the operation of the console. This will ensure that the shot clock operator is able to perform any function quickly and efficiently. During the pre-game checks, the shot clock operator should check the following:

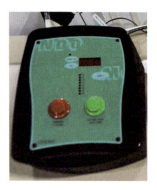

- **Verify if the shot clock count is electronically linked to the game clock.** This means that the shot clock operator needs to know if the shot clock will operate independently of the game clock. The shot clock should be able to be started separately from the game clock.

- **Timeliness of start and stop.**

- **Full second / empty second and sound signal.** According to the rules, the sound should be different from the sound of the game clock. To verify the loudness of the sound signal, the shot clock operator will run down the shot clock to zero when the officials are present on the court in the 20-minute interval of play before the game begins. This will also allow the officials and Table Officials to know if the buzzer sounds when the display reaches zero (empty second), or if it sounds after a further full second has elapsed.

- 以整秒显示，并在最后 5 秒时以 1/10 秒显示。
- 安装在每个篮板后方篮架的支撑物上或悬吊在天花板上。
- 进攻计时钟上的进攻时间数字为红色,同步比赛计时钟的数字为黄色。
- 进攻计时钟上的进攻时间数字最小高度为 230 毫米，并应大于同步比赛计时钟的数字。
- 符合比赛主办国家对电磁兼容性的法定要求。

　　当前进攻计时钟操作面板的种类多样性使得比赛开始前（检查设备期间和赛前的比赛休息期间）花一些时间检查进攻计时钟设备变得格外重要，为的是熟悉设备的操作面板。这样可以确保进攻计时员快速、高效地应用该设备的所有功能。在赛前的检查环节中，进攻计时员应当按照如下步骤检查设备：

- **核实进攻计时钟与比赛计时钟的电子信号是否相连**。也就是说，进攻计时员需要清楚进攻计时钟的操作是否是独立的。进攻计时钟应可以独立于比赛计时钟被开动。
- **开动和停止的时机**。
- **完整的进攻时间周期、进攻时间周期结束和声音信号**。根据规则，进攻计时钟的声音信号应与比赛计时钟的声音信号不同。为了区别两种声音信号，进攻计时员需要在赛前 20 分钟的比赛休息期间，且裁判员在场时，将进攻计时钟倒计时至 0 秒，以确认进攻计时钟的声音信号。这样做，也可以使裁判员和记录台人员知道,进攻计时钟的蜂鸣器是在 0 秒(空秒)时响起的，还是在 0 秒之后又走过一定时间才响起的。

- Whether it is possible to switch the display off so that the shot clock displays are blank (showing no digits).

- Blank - reset to 24 / 14 seconds - START procedure (when the ball touches the ring).

- The devices screens should have the red dot as shown in the image. This dot should only be visible when the game time is stopped. It is a quick way to detect that the time is not working well (especially when using the whistle-controlled time system).

- Check if the shot clock sound signal can be stopped by a new reset (24 / 14) and if it is possible to restart the shot clock immediately after the buzzer has sounded.

- Whether the shot clock can be reset to 14 when less than 24 seconds but more than 14 are left in an offence.

- **Check if the display can be switched off** when less than 24 seconds or 14 seconds are left in a quarter.

- **Whether it is possible to correct the shot clock displays in the case of error,** and if so, which procedure must be used.

7.4 THE RULE

7.4.1 SHOT CLOCK

Application of the 24 seconds rule is an extremely complex task that requires a deep knowledge of the rules and interpretations, a high degree of concentration and the ability to evaluate each situation in tenths of seconds, hundreds of times in a game.

To perform this task properly it is essential to have a perfect knowledge of when team control begins and ends.

7.4.2 CONTROL OF THE BALL

Team control starts when a player of that team is in control of a live ball by holding or dribbling it or a live ball is at team's disposal.

- 查看进攻计时钟是否可以关闭显示，使其清屏（不显示任何数字）。
- 清屏——复位到 24 秒 /14 秒——开动程序（当球接触篮圈时）。
- 进攻计时钟的操作面板屏幕上应当显示如图所示的红点。该红点只有在比赛时间被停止时才亮起。这是一种便捷的方法，用以观察比赛时间是否正常运行（尤其在使用哨声控制计时系统的比赛中）。

- 查看进攻计时钟在被复位（到 24 秒 /14 秒）时，声音信号能否被停止。并且查看在蜂鸣器响后，进攻计时钟能否迅速被开动。
- 查看进攻计时钟能否在进攻时间少于 24 秒、多于 14 秒的情况下，复位到 14 秒。
- 查看进攻计时钟在一节比赛时间少于 24 秒或少于 14 秒的情况下，能否被关闭。
- 查看进攻计时钟在出现错误的情况下能否被更正，如果可以，则必须使用哪一种程序。

7.4 规则

7.4.1 进攻计时钟

执行 24 秒规则是一项极其复杂的工作，这项工作要求进攻计时员必须十分熟悉规则和规则解释，并能够高度集中注意力，且有能力在整场比赛中数百次地在 1/10 秒内评估每一个比赛情况。

为了准确执行这一任务，进攻计时员必须清楚地知道球队何时开始控制球，以及何时结束控制球。

7.4.2 控制球

球队控制球开始于该队一名队员正拿着或运着一个活球，或者可处理一个活球时。

Team control continues when:

- A player of that team is in control of a live ball.
- The ball is being passed between teammates.

Team control ends when:

- An opponent gains control.
- The ball becomes dead.
- The ball has left the player's hand(s) on a shot for a field goal or for a free throw.

7.4.3 THE SHOT CLOCK COUNT

7.4.3.1 THE SHOT CLOCK COUNT SHALL BE STARTED OR RESTARTED WHEN:

- A player gains control of a live ball on the playing court. The mere touching of the ball by an opponent does not start a new shot clock period if the same team remains in control of the ball.

- On a throw-in, the ball touches or is legally touched by any player on the playing court.

A team must attempt a shot for a field goal within 24 seconds.

To constitute a shot for a field goal within 24 seconds:

球队继续控制球，当：

- 某队一名队员控制一个活球时。
- 球在同队队员之间传递时。

球队控制球结束，当：

- 一名对方队员获得控制球时。
- 球成死球时。
- 在投篮或罚球中，球已经离开队员的手时。

7.4.3 进攻计时钟的计时

7.4.3.1 开动或重新开动进攻计时钟，当：

- 某队的一名队员在场上控制活球时。此后对方队员仅仅是接触球，而原控制球队依然控制球时，则不开始一个新的进攻时间周期。

- 在掷球入界中，球接触任一场上队员或被任一场上队员合法接触时。

球队必须在 24 秒内尝试投篮。

一次 24 秒内投篮的构成：

- The ball must leave the player's hand(s) before the shot clock signal sounds, and

- after the ball has left the player's hand(s), the ball must touch the ring or enter the basket.

When a shot for a field goal is attempted near the end of the 24-second period and the shot clock signal sounds while the ball is in the air:

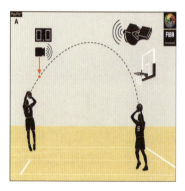

A) If the ball misses the ring, a violation has occurred. However, if the opponents gain immediate and clear control of the ball (B) the signal shall be disregarded and the game shall continue.

C) If the ball enters the basket, no violation has occurred, the signal shall be disregarded and the goal shall count.

D) If the ball touches the ring but does not enter the basket, no violation has occurred, the signal shall be disregarded and the game shall continue.

When the backboard is equipped with yellow lighting along its perimeter at the top, the lighting takes precedence over the shot clock signal sound.

- 在进攻计时钟的信号发出前，球必须离开队员的手。
- 球离开了队员的手后，必须接触篮圈或进入球篮。

在临近 24 秒结束时尝试了一次投篮，并且球在空中时进攻计时钟信号响：

A) 如果球未碰篮圈，一次违例发生。然而，如果对方队员立即和清晰地获得了控制球，B) 信号应被忽略并且比赛应继续。

C) 如果球进入球篮，没有违例发生，信号应被忽略并且计中篮得分。

D) 如果球接触篮圈但未进入球篮，没有违例发生，信号应被忽略并且比赛应继续。

当篮板上沿装有黄色光带时，光带信号亮先于进攻计时钟信号响。

7.4.3.2 SHOT CLOCK COUNT SHALL BE STOPPED, BUT NOT RESET:

with the remaining time visible, when the same team that previously had control of the ball is awarded a throw-in as a result of:

- A ball having gone out-of-bounds.
- A player of the same team having been injured.
- A technical foul committed by that team.
- A jump ball situation.
- A double foul.
- A cancellation of equal penalties against both teams.

Stopped, but also not reset, with the remaining time visible, when the same team that previously had control of the ball is awarded a frontcourt throw-in and 14 or more seconds are displayed on the shot clock as a result of a foul or violation.

The game being stopped because of an action connected with the team in control of the ball.	The game being stopped because of an action not connected with either team. Unless the opponents would be placed at a disadvantage.	The team controlling the ball takes the throw-in after the ball having gone out-of-bounds.	L2M Time-out Head coach's option: to take the throw-in from the frontcourt with 13 or less seconds of possession.	A technical foul is committed by the team in control of the ball.

7.4.3.3 SHALL BE STOPPED, AND RESET TO 24 SECONDS :

with no display visible, when:

- The ball legally enters the basket.
- The ball touches the ring of the opponent's basket and it is controlled by the team that was not in control of the ball before it has touched the ring.
- The team is awarded a backcourt throw-in:
  - As the result of a foul or violation (not for the ball having gone out-of-bounds).

7.4.3.2 停止但不复位进攻计时钟：

在剩余时间可见的情况下，当因以下原因判给原控制球的队掷球入界时：

- 球出界。
- 一名同队队员受伤。
- 该队发生技术犯规。
- 一次跳球情况。
- 一次双方犯规。
- 判给双方球队的相同罚则相互抵消。

当判给原控制球队掷球入界，并且由于犯规或违例而在进攻计时钟上显示14秒或更多时，停止但不复位进攻计时钟，且剩余时间可见。

比赛因与控制球队有关的行为被停止。	比赛因与双方都无关的行为被停止，除非对方会被置于不利。	在球出界后，由原控制球队掷球入界。	进攻时间剩余13秒或更少时，在最后两分钟内的暂停后，主教练选择在前场执行掷球入界。	宣判了一起控制球队的技术犯规。

7.4.3.3 停止进攻计时钟并复位到24秒：

在不显示进攻时间的情况下，当：

- 球合法地进入球篮。
- 球接触对方球篮的篮圈，并且控制球的球队不是球接触篮圈前的控制球队。
- 某队获得后场掷球入界球权：
  - ◆ 作为一次犯规或违例的结果（球出界除外）。

- As the result of a jump ball situation the ball for the team not previously in control of the ball.

- The game is stopped because of an action not connected with the team in control of the ball.

- The game is stopped because of an action not connected with either team, unless the opponents would be placed at a disadvantage.

- The team is awarded free throw(s).

24	**24**	**24**
A new team gains control of a live ball on the playing court.	To take the throw-in after a Basket.	To take the throw-in from the backcourt after a foul or violation by the opponent team.

7.4.3.4 SHALL BE STOPPED, AND RESET TO 14 SECONDS :

with 14 display visible, when:

- The same team that previously had control of the ball is awarded a frontcourt throw-in and 13 seconds or less are displayed on the shot clock:

  - As the result of a foul or violation (not for the ball having gone out-of- bounds).

  - The game being stopped because of an action not connected with the team in control of the ball.

  - The game being stopped because of an action not connected with either team, unless the opponents would be placed at a disadvantage.

- The team that previously did not have the control of the ball shall be awarded a frontcourt throw-in as a result of a:

  - Personal foul or violation (including for the ball having gone out-of-bounds),

  - Jump ball situation.

- A team shall be awarded a throw-in from the throw-in line in its frontcourt as a result of an unsportsmanlike or disqualifying foul.

- ◆ 作为跳球情况的结果，球队先前没有控制球。
- ◆ 比赛因与控制球队无关的行为被停止。
- ◆ 比赛因与双方都无关的行为被停止，除非对方会被置于不利。
- ● 某队获得罚球。

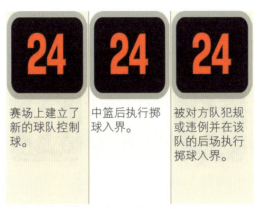

赛场上建立了新的球队控制球。

中篮后执行掷球入界。

被对方队犯规或违例并在该队的后场执行掷球入界。

7.4.3.4 停止进攻计时钟并复位到 14 秒：

在 14 秒可见的情况下，当：

- ● 判给原控制球队在前场掷球入界并且进攻计时钟显示 13 秒或更少：
  - ◆ 作为一次犯规或违例的结果（球出界除外）。
  - ◆ 比赛因与控制球队无关的行为被停止。
  - ◆ 比赛因与双方都无关的行为被停止，除非对方会被置于不利。
- ● 作为一个结果，之前未控制球的队应在前场掷球入界：
  - ◆ 侵人犯规或违例（包括出界）。
  - ◆ 跳球情况。
- ● 作为一次违反体育运动精神的犯规或取消比赛资格的犯规的结果，从该队前场掷球入界线处执行掷球入界。

- After the ball has touched the ring on an unsuccessful shot for a field goal, a last free throw, or on a pass, if the team which regains control of the ball is the same team that was in control of the ball before the ball touched the ring.

- The game clock shows 2:00 minutes or less in the fourth quarter or in each overtime following a time-out taken by the team that is entitled to the possession of the ball from its backcourt and the head coach decides that the game shall be resumed with a throw-in from the throw-in line in the team's frontcourt and 14 seconds or more are displayed on the shot clock at the time when the game clock was stopped.

14	14	14	14	14
The same team recovers ball control after an unsuccessful shot (ball touches the ring) offensive rebound.	To take the throw-in from the frontcourt (off. team) after a foul or violation (including for the ball having gone out-of-bounds) by the opponent team if the remaining time on shot clock is 13 or less seconds.	To take the throw-in from the frontcourt (def. team) after a foul or violation by the team in control of the ball.	To take the throw-in from the throw-in line in the team's frontcourt for a UF / DF penalty.	To take the throw-in from the frontcourt due to the coach's decision during the last 2 minutes of the 4th quarter or overtime if the remaining time on the shot clock is 14 or more seconds.

- 在一次不成功投篮、最后一次不成功的罚球或者一次传球，球接触篮圈后，如果重新控制球的队和球接触篮圈前控制球的队是同一队。
- 第 4 节或每一决胜期比赛计时钟显示 2:00 分钟或更少，后场拥有球权的队请求了一次暂停，主教练决定比赛由该队从其前场掷球入界线处掷球入界重新开始，且比赛计时钟停止时进攻计时钟显示 14 秒或更多。

14	14	14	14	14
在一次不成功投篮（球接触篮圈）后，同一队重新获得了进攻篮板控制球。	进攻队因对方的一起犯规或违例（球出界除外）而在前场掷球入界，并且进攻计时钟显示 13 秒或更少。	防守队因控制球队的一起犯规或违例而在前场掷球入界。	作为一次违反体育运动精神的犯规或取消比赛资格的犯规的结果，从该队前场掷球入界线处执行掷球入界。	第 4 节或每一决胜期比赛计时钟显示 2:00 分钟或更少，后场拥有球权的队请求了一次暂停，主教练决定比赛由该队从其前场掷球入界线处掷球入界重新开始，且比赛计时钟停止时进攻计时钟显示 14 秒或更多。

7.4.3.5 SHALL BE STOPPED, AND SWITCHED OFF:

After the ball becomes dead and the game clock has been stopped in any quarter or overtime when there is a new control of the ball for either team and there are fewer than 14 seconds on the game clock.

The shot clock signal does not stop the game clock or the game, nor causes the ball to become dead, unless a team is in a control of the ball.

7.4.4 SHOT CLOCK OPERATOR SITUATIONS

**SHOT CLOCK AFTER
BALL LODGED BETWEEN THE RING
AND THE BACKBOARD**

- 24 SECONDS for the Team that did not control the ball.

- 14 SECONDS for the Team that controlled the ball.

**SHOT CLOCK AFTER
Unsportsmanlike Foul /
Disqualifying Foul**
All throw-ins part of a UF or DQ penalty shall be administered from the throw-in line in the team's frontcourt, with 14 SECONDS on the shot clock.

7.4.3.5 停止并关闭进攻计时钟：

在任一节或决胜期中，每当球成死球并且比赛计时钟停止时，任一队获得新的控制球，并且比赛计时钟显示少于 14 秒，应关闭进攻计时钟。

进攻计时钟的信号既不停止比赛计时钟或比赛，也不使球成死球（某队正控制球除外）。

7.4.4 进攻计时的情况

球夹在篮圈和篮板之间后的进攻计时

- 非原控制球队拥有球权则复位至 24 秒。
- 原控制球队拥有球权则复位至 14 秒。

违反体育运动精神 / 取消比赛资格的犯规后的进攻计时

属于违反体育运动精神 / 取消比赛资格的犯规罚则一部分的掷球入界应在前场的掷球入界线执行，进攻计时钟应复位至 14 秒。

SHOT CLOCK AFTER
OFFENSIVE FOUL / VIOLATION / BASKET
IN THE FRONTCOURT BY OFFENSIVE
TEAM

Team B throw-in in the backcourt, with 24 SECONDS on the shot clock.

SHOT CLOCK AFTER
OFFENSIVE FOUL / VIOLATION / OUT-
OF-BOUNDS IN THE BACKCOURT BY
OFFENSIVE TEAM

Team B throw-in in the frontcourt, with 14 SECONDS on the shot clock.

SHOT CLOCK AFTER
DEFENSIVE FOUL / VIOLATION
IN THE FRONTCOURT BY DEFENSIVE
TEAM

If 14 seconds or more was shown on the shot clock at the time when the game was stopped, the shot clock shall not be reset, but shall continue from the time it was stopped.

进攻队在其前场被宣判犯规 / 违例 / 中篮后的进攻计时
B 队在其后场掷球入界，进攻计时钟应复位至 24 秒。

新的进攻方向

进攻队在其后场被宣判犯规 / 违例 / 球出界后的进攻计时
B 队在其前场掷球入界，进攻计时钟应复位至 14 秒。

新的进攻方向

防守队在其前场被宣判犯规 / 违例后的进攻计时
如果比赛停止时进攻计时钟显示 14 秒或更多，进攻计时钟不应复位，而是应从剩余时间处连续计算。

SHOT CLOCK AFTER
DEFENSIVE FOUL / VIOLATION
(except Out-of-Bounds)
IN THE FONTCOURT
BY DEFENSIVE TEAM

If 13 seconds or less were shown on the shot clock at the time when the game was stopped, the shot clock shall be reset to 14 seconds.

SHOT CLOCK AFTER
THE GAME IS STOPPED BY A REFEREE

For any reason not connected with either team and, in the judgement of a referee, a reset would place the opponents at a disadvantage, the shot clock shall continue from the time it was stopped.

SHOT CLOCK AFTER
TECHNICAL FOUL BY
THE TEAM IN CONTROL OF THE BALL

Throw-in Backcourt
NO RESET, the SC shall continue from the time it was stopped.

Throw-in Frontcourt
NO RESET, the SC shall continue from the time it was stopped.

SHOT CLOCK AFTER
TECHNICAL FOUL BY
THE TEAM NOT IN CONTROL
OF THE BALL

Throw-in Backcourt
24 SECONDS
Throw-in Frontcourt

- NO RESET if the SC shows 14 sec or more.

- 14 SECONDS if the SC shows 13 sec or less.

防守队在其前场被宣判犯规 / 违例后（除球出界之外）的进攻计时

如果比赛停止时进攻计时钟显示 13 秒或更少，则应复位至 14 秒。

裁判员停止比赛后的进攻计时

因与任一队都无关的原因停止比赛，且根据裁判员的判断，对方队将被置于不利，进攻计时钟不应复位，而是应从剩余时间处连续计算。

SHOT CLOCK AFTER
TECHNICAL FOUL BY
THE TEAM IN CONTROL OF THE BALL
Throw-in Backcourt
NO RESET, the SC shall continue from
the time it was stopped.
Throw-in Frontcourt
NO RESET, the SC shall continue from
the time it was stopped.

SHOT CLOCK AFTER
TECHNICAL FOUL BY
THE TEAM NOT IN CONTROL
OF THE BALL
Throw-in Backcourt
24 SECONDS
Throw-in Frontcourt

- NO RESET if the SC shows
  14 sec or more.

- 14 SECONDS if the SC shows
  13 sec or less.

SHOT CLOCK AFTER
TECHNICAL FOUL
NO TEAM IS IN CONTROL OF THE BALL
JUMP BALL SITUATION
Throw-in Backcourt
24 SECONDS.
Throw-in Frontcourt
14 SECONDS.

SHOT CLOCK AFTER
FIGHTING (Art.39) WITH ALL
PENALTIES CANCELLING EACH OTHER,
OR AFTER A DOUBLE FOUL
The team which was in the control of
the ball or was entitled to the ball when
the fight began or when the double foul
occurred, shall be awarded a throw-in
from the place nearest to where the ball
was located when the fight/double foul
occurred.
The team shall have the remaining time
on the SC when the game was stopped.

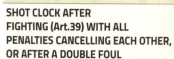
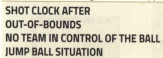

SHOT CLOCK AFTER
OUT-OF-BOUNDS
NO TEAM IN CONTROL OF THE BALL
JUMP BALL SITUATION
Throw-in Backcourt
24 SECONDS.
Throw-in Frontcourt
14 SECONDS.

SHOT CLOCK AFTER
OUT OF BOUNDS
CAUSED BY TEAM "A"
THROW-IN FOR TEAM "B"
Throw-in Backcourt
24 SECONDS.
Throw-in Frontcourt
14 SECONDS.

宣判一起技术犯规时，没有球队控制球，出现跳球情况的进攻计时

在后场执行掷球入界
复位至 24 秒。
在前场执行掷球入界
复位至 14 秒。

在一起打架（规则第 39 条）或一起双方犯规中抵消了双方球队的相同罚则后的进攻计时

某队已控制球或拥有球权，应将球判给该队从打架开始时或双方犯规发生时距离球最近的地点执行掷球入界。
该队应拥有比赛停止时进攻计时钟的剩余时间。

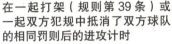

球出界后，没有球队控制球，出现跳球情况的进攻计时

在后场执行掷球入界
复位至 24 秒。
在前场执行掷球入界
复位至 14 秒。

"A" 队导致球出界后，由 "B" 队掷球入界的进攻计时

在后场执行掷球入界
复位至 24 秒。
在前场执行掷球入界
复位至 14 秒。

SHOT CLOCK AFTER OUT-OF-BOUNDS CAUSED BY TEAM "B" THROW-IN FOR TEAM "A"

Throw-in Backcourt & **Throw-in Frontcourt**

NO RESET, the SC shall continue from the time it was stopped.

SHOT CLOCK AFTER TIME-OUT L2M

Throw-in Backcourt

- Out of bounds: NO RESET the SC shall continue from the time it was stopped.
- Basket / Foul / Other Violation the SC shall be RESET to 24 SECONDS.

Throw-in Frontcourt

- 14 SECONDS if SC shows 14 or more.
- NO RESET if SC shows 13 or less.

SHOT CLOCK AFTER JUMP BALL SITUATION NO TEAM IS IN CONTROL OF THE BALL

Throw-in Backcourt
24 SECONDS.
Throw-in Frontcourt
14 SECONDS.

SHOT CLOCK AFTER JUMP BALL SITUATION TEAM A CONTROL THE BALL THROW-IN FOR TEAM A

IF THE ARROW FAVOURS TEAM A
NO RESET, the SC shall continue from the time it was stopped.

IF THE ARROW FAVOURS TEAM B
Throw-in for TEAM B from its Backcourt
24 SECONDS.
Throw-in for TEAM B from its Frontcourt
14 SECONDS.

"B"队导致球出界后，由"A"队掷球入界
在后场和前场执行掷球入界
进攻计时钟不应复位，而是应从剩余时间处连续计算。

最后 2 分钟内，一次暂停后的进攻计时
在后场执行掷球入界
- 球出界：进攻计时钟不应复位，而是应从剩余时间处连续计算。
- 中篮/犯规/其他违例：进攻计时钟应复位至 24 秒。

在前场执行掷球入界
- 如果进攻计时钟显示 14 秒或更多，进攻计时钟应复位至 14 秒。
- 如果进攻计时钟显示 13 秒或更少，则不应复位。

出现跳球情况，没有球队控制球的进攻计时
在后场执行掷球入界
复位至 24 秒。
在前场执行掷球入界
复位至 14 秒。

A 队控制球时出现跳球情况，判给 A 队掷球入界的进攻计时
如果交替拥有箭头指向 A 队，进攻计时钟不应复位，而是应从剩余时间处连续计算。
如果交替拥有箭头指向 B 队，
在 B 队的后场执行掷球入界
复位至 24 秒。
在 B 队的前场执行掷球入界
复位至 14 秒。

7.4.5 EXAMPLES OF 24/14 SECONDS WHEN THE SHOT CLOCK SIGNAL SOUNDS

SITUATIONS WHEN THE SHOT CLOCK SIGNAL SOUNDS						
	Ball in the hand	Signal sounds by mistake	Ball in the air			
			Enters the basket (valid field goal)	Touches the ring and rebounds	Does not touch the ring & no immediate defensive control	Does not touch the ring & immediate defensive control
What should the referee do?	Call	No call	No call	No call	Call	No call
Decision						

SHOT CLOCK SITUATIONS WITH SHOT FOR FIELD GOAL			
	1	Team A shot released. The ball enters the basket - display blanked.	Basket counts. Ball for Team B, from the endline, new 24 seconds.
	2	Team A shot released. The ball touches the ring but does not enter the basket - display blanked.	Rebound for Team B, new 24 seconds. Rebound for Team A, new 14 seconds.
SHOT FOR FIELD GOAL	3	Team A shot released. The ball does not touch the ring. Team A remains in control of the ball.	Shot clock continues.
	4	Team A shot released. The ball does not touch the ring. Team B gains the control of the ball.	New shot-clock period, 24 seconds, for Team B.
	5	Ball passing between Team A players or ball deflected by either team. The ball touches the ring - display blanked.	Team B gains control, new 24 seconds. Team A remains in control, new 14 seconds.

7.4.5 24 秒或 14 秒进攻计时钟信号响的举例

进攻计时钟信号响时的不同情况						
	球在手中	信号错响	球在空中			
			进入球篮（中篮得分）	接触篮圈并弹起	未接触篮圈且防守队未立即获得控制球	未接触篮圈但防守队立即获得控制球
裁判员应如何宣判？	宣判	不宣判	不宣判	不宣判	宣判	不宣判
决定						

试投后的不同情况下进攻计时钟的操作				
试投	1	A 队投篮出手 球进入球篮，进攻计时钟清屏	中篮有效 由 B 队在端线掷球入界，拥有新的 24 秒周期	
	2	A 队投篮出手 球接触篮圈但未进入球篮，进攻计时钟清屏	如 B 队得到篮板球，拥有新的 24 秒周期 如 A 队得到篮板球，拥有新的 14 秒周期	
	3	A 队投篮出手 球未接触篮圈 随后 A 队继续控制球	进攻计时钟连续计算	
	4	A 队投篮出手 球未接触篮圈 随后 B 队获得控制球	B 队拥有一个新的 24 秒周期	
	5	球在 A 队队员之间传递或任一队队员接触了球 随后球接触篮圈，进攻计时钟清屏	如 B 队得到控制球，拥有新的 24 秒周期 如 A 队继续控制球，拥有新的 14 秒周期	

SIGNAL SOUNDS WHEN THE BALL IS IN THE AIR FOR A SHOT	**6**	Team A shot released. The ball touches the ring with more than 14 seconds on the shot clock - display blanked. Team A gets the rebound.	The shot clock shall be reset to 14 seconds when Team A gets the rebound .
	7	Team A shot released. Shot clock signal sounds. The ball enters the basket, display blanked.	Basket counts. Throw-in for Team B from the endline, new 24 seconds.
	8	Team A shot released. Shot clock signal sounds. The ball touches the backboard. The ball enters the basket - display blanked.	Basket counts. Throw-in for Team B from the endline, new 24 seconds.
	9	Team A shot released. Shot clock signal sounds. The ball touches the ring - display blanked. The ball enters the basket.	Basket counts. Throw-in for Team B from the endline, new 24 seconds.
	10	Team A shot released. Shot clock signal sounds. The ball touches the ring - display blanked. The ball does not enter the basket.	Team B gains control, new 24 seconds. Team A gains control, new 14 seconds.
	11	Team A shot released. Shot clock signal sounds. The ball does not touch the ring. Rebound for Team A.	Shot clock violation. Throw-in for Team B, new 24 seconds.
	12	Team A shot released. Shot clock signal sounds. The ball does not touch the ring. Both teams fight for the rebound.	Shot clock violation. Throw-in Team B, new 24 seconds.
	13	Team A shot released. Shot clock signal sounds. The ball does not touch the ring. Rebound and immediate control for Team B.	No violation. Team B has new 24 seconds.
	14	Team A shot released. Shot clock signal sounds. The ball touches the ring – display blanked and then is touched by Team A or Team B. before it goes out-of-bounds.	Throw-in for Team B, new 24 seconds / Throw-in for Team A, new 14 seconds .

球在空中时信号响起	6	A队投篮出手 进攻时间多于14秒时球接触篮圈，进攻计时钟清屏 A队得到篮板球	当A队得到篮板球时，进攻计时钟应复位至14秒
	7	A队投篮出手 进攻计时钟信号响起 球进入球篮，进攻计时钟清屏	中篮有效 由B队在端线掷球入界，拥有新的24秒周期
	8	A队投篮出手 进攻计时钟信号响起 球接触篮板 球进入球篮，进攻计时钟清屏	中篮有效 由B队在端线掷球入界，拥有新的24秒周期
	9	A队投篮出手 进攻计时钟信号响起 球接触篮圈，进攻计时钟清屏 球进入球篮	中篮有效 由B队在端线掷球入界，拥有新的24秒周期
	10	A队投篮出手 进攻计时钟信号响起 球接触篮圈，进攻计时钟清屏 球未进入球篮	如B队获得控制球，拥有新的24秒周期 如A队获得控制球，拥有新的14秒周期
	11	A队投篮出手 进攻计时钟信号响起 球未接触篮圈 A队得到篮板球	进攻时间违例 由B队掷球入界，拥有新的24秒周期
	12	A队投篮出手 进攻计时钟信号响起 球未接触篮圈 双方球队争抢篮板球	进攻时间违例 由B队掷球入界，拥有新的24秒周期
	13	A队投篮出手 进攻计时钟信号响起 球未接触篮圈 篮板球，B队立即控制球	未发生进攻时间违例 B队拥有新的24秒周期
	14	A队投篮出手 进攻计时钟信号响起 球接触篮圈，进攻计时钟清屏 球被A队或B队接触后出界	如B队掷球入界，拥有新的24秒周期 如A队掷球入界，拥有新的14秒周期

SHOT FOR FIELD GOAL, THE BALL TOUCHES THE RING & THE SHOT CLOCK SIGNAL SOUNDS	15	Team A shot released. The ball enters the basket. Shot clock signal sounds.	The shot clock signal sounds in error. The signal is ignored and the basket counts. Throw-in for Team B, new 24 seconds.
	16	Team A shot released. The ball touches the ring. Team A / B gains control of the ball. Shot clock signal sounds.	The shot clock signal sounds in error. The signal is ignored and the game continues.
	17	Team A shot released. The ball touches the ring. Shot clock signal sounds. The referee blows the whistle in error.	The game is stopped by a referee. No Team has control of the ball. Jump ball situation - use direction arrow. If Team A = 14 seconds; if Team B = 24 seconds.
SHOT FOR FIELD GOAL, THE SHOT CLOCK SIGNAL SOUNDS & GOALTENDING OR BLOCKED SHOT	18	Team A shot released. Shot clock signal sounds. The ball is on its upward flight to the basket and then touched by Team A or B and does not touch the ring.	Shot clock violation. Throw-in for Team B at the place nearest to the ball at the violation, new 24 seconds.
	19	Team A shot released. Shot clock signal sounds. The ball is on its downward flight to the basket and then touched by Team A.	Team A goaltending violation - display blanked. Throw-in for Team B at the free-throw line extended, new 24 seconds.
	20	Team A shot released. Shot clock signal sounds. The ball is on its downward flight to the basket and then touched by Team B.	Goaltending violation, basket counts - display blanked. Throw-in for Team B at the endline, new 24 seconds.

投篮出手的球接触篮圈，进攻计时钟信号响起	15	A队投篮出手 球进入球篮 进攻计时钟信号响起	进攻计时钟误响 应忽略信号且得分有效 由B队掷球入界，拥有新的24秒周期
	16	A队投篮出手 球接触篮圈 A队或B队获得控制球 进攻计时钟信号响起	进攻计时钟误响 应忽略信号且比赛继续
	17	A队投篮出手 球接触篮圈 进攻计时钟信号响起 裁判员误鸣哨	比赛被裁判员停止 没有球队控制球 跳球情况，应使用交替拥有箭头 如指向A队，14秒；如指向B队，24秒；
投篮出手，进攻计时钟信号响起，发生干涉得分或封盖	18	A队投篮出手 进攻计时钟信号响起 球在向上飞向球篮过程中被A队或B队接触，随后球未接触篮圈	进攻时间违例 由B队在违例发生时最靠近球的位置掷球入界，拥有新的24秒周期
	19	A队投篮出手 进攻计时钟信号响起 球在下落飞向球篮过程中被A队接触	A队干涉得分违例，进攻计时钟清屏 由B队在罚球线的延长线掷球入界，拥有新的24秒周期
	20	A队投篮出手 进攻计时钟信号响起 球在下落飞向球篮过程中被B队接触	干涉得分违例，应计得分，进攻计时钟清屏 由B队在端线掷球入界，拥有新的24秒周期

SHOT FOR FIELD GOAL, THE SHOT CLOCK SIGNAL SOUNDS & GOALTENDING OR BLOCKED SHOT

#		
21	Team A shot released. The ball is legally blocked by Team B. Shot clock signal sounds. The ball enters the basket.	Basket counts. Throw-in for Team B at the endline, new 24 seconds.
22	Team A shot released. The ball is legally blocked by Team B Shot clock signal sounds. The ball does not enter the basket or touch the ring.	Shot clock violation. Throw-in for Team B, at the endline with new 24 seconds, unless Team B gets clear and immediate control of the ball.
23	Team A shot released. The ball is legally blocked by Team B . Shot clock signal sounds. The ball goes out-of-bounds.	Shot clock violation. Throw-in for the Team B at the endline with the new 24 seconds.
24	Team A shot. The ball is legally blocked by Team B . Team B gets control of the ball. Shot clock signal sounds .	The shot clock signal sounds in error. The signal is ignored and the game continues. New 24 seconds for Team B.
25	Team A shot released. The ball is legally blocked by Team B . B1 fouls the shooter. Shot clock signal sounds.	The shot clock signal sounds in error. Free throws for the shooter of Team A. Shot clock blanked.
26	Team A shot released. The ball is legally blocked by Team B. Shot clock signal sounds . B1 fouls the shooter.	Shot clock violation. The foul shall be disregarded unless it is a technical, unsportsmanlike or disqualifying foul. Throw-in for Team B at the place nearest to the infraction, new 24 seconds.

投篮出手，进攻计时钟信号响起，发生干涉得分或封盖	21	A 队投篮出手 球被 B 队合法封盖 进攻计时钟信号响起 球进入球篮	中篮有效 由 B 队在端线掷球入界，拥有新的 24 秒周期
	22	A 队投篮出手 球被 B 队合法封盖 进攻计时钟信号响起 球未进入球篮，也没有接触篮圈	进攻时间违例 由 B 队在端线掷球入界，拥有新的 24 秒周期，除非 B 队立即和清晰地获得了控制球
	23	A 队投篮出手 球被 B 队合法封盖 进攻计时钟信号响起 随后球出界	进攻时间违例 由 B 队在端线掷球入界，拥有新的 24 秒周期
	24	A 队投篮出手 球被 B 队合法封盖 随后 B 队获得控制球 进攻计时钟信号响起	进攻计时钟误响 应忽略信号且比赛继续 B 队拥有新的 24 秒周期
	25	A 队投篮出手 球被 B 队合法封盖 投篮队员被 B1 犯规 进攻计时钟信号响起	进攻计时钟误响 A 队的投篮队员获得罚球 进攻计时钟清屏
	26	A 队投篮出手 球被 B 队合法封盖 进攻计时钟信号响起 投篮队员被 B1 犯规	进攻时间违例 该犯规应被忽略，除非是一起技术的、违反体育运动精神的或取消比赛资格的犯规 由 B 队在最靠近违犯的地点掷球入界，拥有新的 24 秒周期

MISTAKE BY SHOT CLOCK OPERATOR & OTHER SITUATIONS

27	Team A shot released. The ball touches the ring and then Team B gains control of the ball and starts dribbling. Shot clock signal sounds in error and referee blows the whistle.	The referee calls in error. Throw-in for Team B at the place nearest to the ball at the time of the call with the remaining time on the shot clock on Team B's possession.
28	A4 attempts a dunk. The ball touches the ring and returns to the Team A's backcourt. Before a player of either team gains control of the ball, the shot clock signal sounds. Referee did not blow the whistle.	The shot clock signal sounds in error and shall be ignored. The shot clock shall be reset to 14 seconds, if Team A gains possession. 24 seconds, if Team B gains possession.
29	Team A has control of the ball for 20 seconds, when a technical foul is called against A1, followed by another technical foul on B1.	This is a special situation. Both fouls must be cancelled. Throw-in for Team A at the place nearest to the ball at the time of the call with only 4 seconds remaining on the shot clock for Team A.
30	Team A has the ball for 15 seconds and the referee stops the game <ul><li>to get the floor wiped</li><li>because the game clock is not working properly</li><li>because a spectator has entered the court.</li></ul>	In all cases the game continues with a throw-in for Team A with 24 seconds, if it is in Team A's backcourt 14 seconds, if it is in Team A's frontcourt unless the opponent is placed at a disadvantage.

SHOT CLOCK & HELD BALL

31	Team A shot released. Shot clock signal sounds . The ball does not touch the ring, after which, a held ball is immediately called.	Shot clock violation. Throw-in for Team B at the place nearest to the infraction, new 24 seconds.
32	Team A shot released. The ball touches the ring - display blanked, held ball is immediately called.	If Team A is awarded an alternating possession throw-in – 14 seconds. If Team B is awarded an alternating possession throw-in – 24 seconds.
33	Team A shot released. The ball touches the ring -display blanked Then Team A gains control and a held ball is immediately called.	If Team A is awarded an alternating possession throw-in – remaining time on the shot clock (less than 14 seconds.) . If Team B is awarded an alternating possession throw-in – 24 seconds.
34	Team A shot released. The ball touches the ring. then Team B gains control and a held ball is immediately called.	If Team A alternating possession throw-in – new 24 seconds. If Team B is awarded an alternating possession throw-in – remaining time on the shot clock (less than 24 sec).

27	A队投篮出手 球接触篮圈后被B队获得控制球，B队开始运球 进攻计时钟误响，裁判员鸣哨	裁判员因为该误响而鸣哨 由B队在最靠近鸣哨时球所在的位置掷球入界，进攻计时钟应从剩余时间处连续计算
进攻计时员的失误和其他情况 28	A4尝试一次扣篮 球接触篮圈后回到了A队的后场 在任一队员获得控制球之前，进攻计时钟信号响起 裁判员没有鸣哨	进攻计时钟误响且应被忽略。进攻计时钟应复位至： 如A队获得控制球，14秒 如B队获得控制球，24秒
29	A队已控制球20秒，宣判A1一起技术犯规，随后宣判B1一起技术犯规	这是一起特殊情况 这两个犯规必须被抵消 由A队在最靠近鸣哨时球所在的位置掷球入界，A队应只有所剩的4秒进攻时间
30	A队已控制球15秒，裁判员停止比赛，因为： ·要求拖地板 ·比赛计时钟未正确运转 ·一名观众进入了赛场	这些情况下，都应由A队掷球入界： 如果在A队的后场掷球入界，24秒 如果在A队的前场掷球入界，14秒 除非对方会被置于不利
进攻计时钟和争球 31	A队投篮出手 进攻计时钟信号响起 球未接触篮圈，随后，立即宣判了一起争球	进攻时间违例 由B队在最靠近违犯的地点掷球入界，新的24秒周期
32	A队投篮出手 球接触篮圈，进攻计时钟清屏 随后，立即宣判了一起争球	如果交替拥有箭头指向A队，14秒 如果交替拥有箭头指向B队，24秒
33	A队投篮出手 球接触篮圈，进攻计时钟清屏 A队获得控制球，随后立即宣判了一起争球	如果交替拥有箭头指向A队，拥有进攻计时钟剩余的时间（少于14秒） 如果交替拥有箭头指向B队，24秒
34	A队投篮出手 球接触篮圈 随后B队获得控制球，立即宣判了一起争球	如果交替拥有箭头指向A队，24秒 如果交替拥有箭头指向B队，拥有进攻计时钟剩余的时间（少于24秒）

DEFENSIVE FOULS	**35** A1 releases a shot for a field goal. The ball is in the air when 15 seconds are left on the shot clock. B2 fouls A2 – It is Team B's 2nd foul. The ball does not enter the basket.	Throw-in for Team A at the place nearest to the infraction, with 15 seconds remaining on the shot clock .
	36 A1 releases a shot for a field goal The ball is in the air when 10 seconds are left on the shot clock. B2 fouls A2, it is Team B's 2nd foul. The ball does not enter.	Throw-in for Team A at the place nearest to the infraction, with new 14 seconds on the shot clock.
	37 A1 releases a shot for a field goal. The ball is in the air when 10 seconds are left on the shot clock. B2 fouls A2, it is Team B's 2nd foul. The ball enters the basket/touches the ring.	If the ball enters the basket, the basket counts. Team A throw-in at the place nearest to the infraction, with new 14 seconds on the shot clock.
SHOT CLOCK AND VIOLATIONS	**38** Team A in control of the ball in the frontcourt. A travelling /illegal dribble violation has been called.	Throw-in Team B at the place nearest to the infraction, with new 24 seconds on the shot clock.
	39 Team A in control of the ball in the backcourt. A travelling /illegal dribble violation has been called.	Throw-in Team B at the place nearest to the infraction, with new 14 seconds on the shot clock.
	40 Team A throw-in in the frontcourt. A five seconds violation has been called against Team A.	Throw-in Team B at the place nearest to the infraction, with new 24 seconds on the shot clock.
	41 Team A throw-in in the backcourt. A five seconds violation has been called against Team A.	Throw-in Team B at the place nearest to the infraction, with new 14 seconds on the shot clock.
	42 Team A frontcourt throw-in with 16 seconds on the shot clock. B1 in team A's frontcourt deliberately kicks the ball with the foot or strikes the ball with the fist or places the arms over the boundary line and blocks A1's pass.	B1's violation. Throw-in Team A at the place of the infraction (frontcourt) with 16 seconds remaining on shot clock.

防守犯规	35	A1 投篮出手 当球在空中时，进攻计时钟显示 15 秒 B2 对 A2 犯规，这是 B 队的第 2 次犯规 球未进入球篮	由 A 队在最靠近违犯的地点掷球入界，A 队拥有进攻计时钟剩余的 15 秒
	36	A1 投篮出手 当球在空中时，进攻计时钟显示 10 秒 B2 对 A2 犯规，这是 B 队的第 2 次犯规 球未进入球篮	由 A 队在最靠近违犯的地点掷球入界，A 队拥有新的 14 秒周期
	37	A1 投篮出手 当球在空中时，进攻计时钟显示 10 秒 B2 对 A2 犯规，这是 B 队的第 2 次犯规 球进入球篮或接触篮圈	如果球进入了球篮，得分有效 由 A 队在最靠近违犯的地点掷球入界，A 队拥有新的 14 秒周期
进攻计时钟和违例	38	A 队在其前场控制球，宣判了一起带球走或非法运球违例	由 B 队在最靠近违犯的地点掷球入界，B 队拥有新的 24 秒周期
	39	A 队在其后场控制球，宣判了一起带球走或非法运球违例	由 B 队在最靠近违犯的地点掷球入界，B 队拥有新的 14 秒周期
	40	A 队在其前场掷球入界，宣判了 A 队的 5 秒违例	由 B 队在最靠近违犯的地点掷球入界，B 队拥有新的 24 秒周期
	41	A 队在其后场掷球入界，宣判了 A 队的 5 秒违例	由 B 队在最靠近违犯的地点掷球入界，B 队拥有新的 14 秒周期
	42	进攻计时钟显示 16 秒，A 队在其前场掷球入界 B1 在 A 队的前场故意脚踢或拳击球或将手臂越过界线阻拦 A1 的传球	B1 违例 由 A 队在最靠近违犯的地点掷球入界（前场），A 队拥有进攻计时钟剩余的 16 秒

SHOT CLOCK AND VIOLATIONS

| 43 | Team A frontcourt throw-in with 12 seconds on the shot clock.
B1 in team A's frontcourt deliberately kicks the ball with the foot or strikes the ball with the fist or places the arms over the boundary line and blocks A1's pass. | B1's violation.
Throw-in Team A at the place of the infraction (frontcourt) with the shot clock reset to 14 seconds. |
| 44 | Team A backcourt throw-in with 19 seconds on the shot clock.
B1 in team A's backcourt deliberately kicks the ball with the foot or strikes the ball with the fist or places the arms over the boundary line and blocks A1's pass. | B1's violation.
Throw-in Team A at the place of the infraction (backcourt) with new 24 seconds. |

7.5 DURING THE GAME

7.5.1   24" / 14" GUIDELINES

Change of control

For team control to change a defending player must establish control of the ball. This takes place when a player holds the ball (with one or both hands), dribbles the ball or a live ball is at team's disposal. Therefore, a simple touch of the ball by a defensive player is not considered to be a change of team control.

The shot clock operator must be sure that team control has changed before resetting the shot clock.

If a defensive player takes the ball with both hands this is always a change of team control even in a no-look situation as shown in the picture.

进攻计时钟和违例	**43** 进攻计时钟显示 12 秒，A 队在其前场掷球入界 B1 在 A 队的前场故意脚踢或拳击球或将手臂越过界线阻拦 A1 的传球	B1 违例 由 A 队在最靠近违犯的地点掷球入界（前场），进攻计时钟应复位至 14 秒
	44 进攻计时钟显示 19 秒，A 队在其后场掷球入界 B1 在 A 队的后场故意脚踢或拳击球或将手臂越过界线阻拦 A1 的传球	B1 违例 由 A 队在最靠近违犯的地点掷球入界（后场），A 队拥有新的 24 秒周期

7.5 赛中

7.5.1 24 秒和 14 秒的指导方针

球队控制球的改变

只有在防守队员建立对球的控制时，球队控制球才发生改变。这就要求某队员必须拿球（单手或双手），运球，或某队可处理一个活球时。因此，防守队员仅仅接触球并不被视为球队控制球发生了改变。

进攻计时员只有确定球队控制球发生了改变，才可以复位进攻计时钟。

一名防守队员双手拿球的情况始终应被视为球队控制球已发生改变，即便是如图所示的不看球的情况下也是如此。

Team control starts when a player of that team is in control of a live ball by holding or dribbling it or a live ball is at team's disposal.

The shot clock operator must be sure that team control has changed before resetting the shot clock.

If the defensive player takes the ball with both hands (B) or the ball comes to rest in 1 hand (C) it is always a team control and the shot clock shall be reset. (OBRI 14-3 b). Control does not change if the ball is only tapped by 1 hand by the defensive player. Shot clock must continue (OBRI 14-3 a).

(A) No Control of the Ball   (B) Control of the Ball   (C) Control of the Ball

Due to their fixed position on the court, the Table Officials do not always have a clear vision of what is happening on it. Therefore, it is of the utmost importance that they (all Table Officials, not only the shot clock operator) are ready to see and communicate clearly all the referees' signals.

Signals and their meaning

- Fig 3. During a throw-in, the timer and shot clock operator to start their clock.
- Fig 13. Ok, good job.
- Fig 14. Could mean, for example, that team control has been changed or that the ball has touched the ring.

球队控制球开始于该队一名队员正拿着或运着一个活球，或者可处理一个活球时。

　　进攻计时员只有确定球队控制球发生了改变，才可以复位进攻计时钟。

　　如果防守队员双手拿球（B），或球在一只手中停留（C），就总认为是球队控制球，进攻计时钟应被复位（规则解释 14-3b）。如果防守队员仅仅是单手拍击球，球队控制球不发生改变。进攻计时钟必须连续计算（规则解释 14-3a）。

（A）没有控制球　　　　　　（B）控制球　　　　　　（C）控制球

　　由于记录台人员在场边的固定位置就座，他们未必始终拥有可以观察场上所有情况的清晰视角。因此，极为重要的是，他们（指所有的记录台人员，不仅仅是进攻计时员）需要时刻准备着观察裁判员的手势并清晰地与裁判员交流。

　　手势及其意义①

　　图3，掷球入界过程中，计时员和进攻计时员应开动他们的计时钟。

　　图13，好的，做得好。

　　图14，可能意味着，比如：球队控制球已发生改变或球已接触了篮圈。

----

① 以下图号遵照篮球记录台人员手册英文版，参见篮球规则"裁判员手势"。

3 START THE CLOCK	13 COMMUNICATION	14 SHOT CLOCK RESET

Chop with hand	Thumb up	Rotate hand, extend index finger

Fouls and violations except the last 2 minutes

Whenever a whistle is blown, it is important that the shot clock operator does not change the shot clock immediately. The operator should wait until all communications from the referees are completed before making any changes. This is to avoid making mistakes.

- **STOP the shot clock** – when a foul or a violation is called by a referee.
- **RESET** (if necessary, and blank if necessary) - when the referee ends reporting to the table.

The shot clock operator must pay attention and memorise or write down how many seconds are left on display before any reset (conscious reset) takes place, so that he/she can promptly recall it, if necessary.

In the case of violations, the reset (if requested by the rules) must be done at the end of the referees' signalling to the table.

The last 2 minutes or less the 4th quarter or overtime (L2M)

The shot clock operator has to wait for the head coach's decision after a time-out, to see if the coach wants to move the throw-in position from the backcourt to the frontcourt. This will imply to change and adjust the shot clock according to the rule.

After the time-out, the throw-in shall be administered as follows:

Backcourt

- After basket: 24 seconds on the shot clock.
- After foul or violation: 24 seconds on the shot clock.
- After out-of-bounds: if the same team control of the ball, the shot clock operator shall continue from the time it was stopped.

图3 计时开始

用手做砍势

图13 交流

拇指向上

图14 进攻计时钟复位

伸出食指 并转动手

最后 2 分钟之前的犯规和违例

当裁判员鸣哨时，进攻计时员不要立即变动进攻计时钟，这一点非常重要。进攻计时员应等到裁判员结束沟通以后，再做必要的操作。这可以避免发生错误。

- **停止进攻计时钟**：当裁判员鸣哨宣判犯规或违例时。
- **复位**（如需要或清屏）：当裁判员结束向记录台的报告以后。

进攻计时员必须全神贯注，并且记忆或写下复位（有意识的复位）前剩余的进攻时间，此举可以在必要时纠正进攻时间。

发生违例时，复位（依照规则）必须在裁判员结束向记录台完成手势后再操作。

当第 4 节或决胜期还剩最后 2 分钟或更少时（L2M）

在暂停后，进攻计时员必须等待主教练决定比赛重新开始的掷球入界位置（前场还是后场）。该决定将要求进攻计时员根据规则来变动和调节进攻计时钟。

在暂停后，掷球入界应依照下列原则执行：

后场

- 中篮后：进攻计时钟显示 24 秒。
- 犯规或违例后：进攻计时钟显示 24 秒。
- 球出界后：如果原控制球队控制球，进攻计时钟从停止处继续计算。

- After out-of-bounds, if the new offensive team control of the ball, the shot clock be reset to a new 24 seconds on the shot clock.

Frontcourt

- After basket: 14 seconds on the shot clock.

- After foul or violation: 14 seconds on the shot clock.

- After out-of-bounds: 13 seconds or less on the shot clock, if the same team controls the ball, the game shall continue from the time it was stopped.

- After out-of-bounds, 14 seconds or more, if the same team control of the ball, 14 seconds on the shot clock.

Instant Replay Situations (IRS)

When there is an IRS, the shot clock operator should not reset the shot clock until the crew chief has taken the final decision.

Operations - Scoring

Players often surprise us with unexpected shooting actions (alley hoops, tapping or dunking the ball etc.). Be prepared for any possibility, such as the ball not touching the ring, or touching the string / net only. Also, be aware that the ball may become stuck between the ring and the backboard (this is a jump ball situation).

When the ball touches the ring, the rules indicate that the shot clock should be blanked until one of the teams gains control of the ball. Many devices do not allow blanking at all, and on some devices this blanking action is very slow.

If the display can be blanked the shot clock operator should apply the rule fully:

- Blank when the ball touches the opponents' ring.

- Reset to 24 and then start when control is gained by the defending team.

- Reset to 14 and then start when control is gained by the same team that attempted the field goal.

If the display cannot be blanked the shot clock operator shall work as follows:

- Reset the shot clock to 24 seconds when the ball touches the opponents' ring.

- Start the clock count when control is gained by the defending team.

- Reset to 14 and then start the shot clock count when control is gained by the same team that attempted the field goal.

- 球出界后：如果新控制球队控制球，进攻计时钟复位至 24 秒。

前场

- 中篮后：进攻计时钟显示 14 秒。
- 犯规或违例后：进攻计时钟显示 14 秒。
- 球出界后：当进攻计时钟显示 13 秒或更少时，如果原控制球队控制球，进攻计时钟从停止处继续计算。
- 球出界后：当进攻计时钟显示 14 秒或更多时，如果原控制球队控制球，进攻计时钟显示 14 秒。

即时回放系统（IRS）

在使用即时回放系统的比赛中，只有在主裁判员做出最终决定后，进攻计时员才可以复位进攻计时钟。

操作 – 得分时

队员时常会用意想不到的投篮动作（空中接力、拍击、扣篮等）给我们带来惊喜。进攻计时员应随时准备好应对任何可能，例如：球未接触篮圈，或仅接触到网绳或篮网。同样，要注意球也可能夹在篮圈与篮板之间（这是跳球的情况）。

依据规则，当球接触篮圈时，进攻计时钟应清屏，直到某队控制球。许多设备无法实现清屏，而有些设备的清屏功能反应非常慢。

如果进攻计时钟可以实现清屏功能，那么进攻计时员应完全依照如下的规则操作：

- 当球接触对方的篮圈时，进攻计时钟清屏。
- 当防守队获得控制球时，复位至 24 秒。
- 当试投的同一队获得控制球时，复位至 14 秒。

如果进攻计时钟无法实现清屏，那么进攻计时员应依照如下内容操作：

- 当球接触对方的篮圈时，进攻计时钟复位至 24 秒。
- 当防守队获得控制球时，开动进攻计时钟。
- 当试投的同一队获得控制球时，先复位至 14 秒，随即开动进攻计时钟。

It is important to note that some shot clock devices do not stop counting when the display is blanked. It is crucial the shot clock operator finds out if this is the case as part of the pre-game checks. This will avoid situations like, for example, having the shot clock signal sound during free throws (when the shot clock should be blanked).

If blanking the shot clock takes too long and causes a delay in the application of the rule, then the shot clock must not be blanked. In this case, the previous working method must be followed, which is used when the shot clock cannot be blanked.

7.5.2 MECHANICS SUMMARY

The shot clock operator's duties require a continuous concentration on the ball, especially when the ball is close to be released for a shot for a goal and when it is about to touch the ring. For this reason, it is very important not to be afraid of sounding the shot clock in these extreme situations.

According to the FIBA rules, the sounding of the shot clock device should not stop the game clock.

- **Check the device thoroughly** in your pre-game checks.

- **Familiarise yourself with its operation** in your pre-game checks and in the interval of play before tip-off.

- **You must always have your hands on the device console**, close to the operational buttons / levers, and not on the table. This is necessary because tenths of seconds may mean the difference between a field goal scored or not, as well as a game won or lost.

- **The whole table officiating team must have a good vision of the shot clock devices.**

- **Before each reset, memorise how many seconds are left, especially in the L2M and IRS,** in order to promptly recall the time if necessary.

- **Stay focused on the ball,** especially during shot attempts.

- **The excellent shot clock operator** is the person who can find the right balance between the ability to react quickly and self-control, to ensure the accuracy and timeliness of the application of the rule.

- **To avoid any mistakes, it is better to hold the display of the shot clock before a change in team control.** To avoid confusion, first press the stop button whenever the ball goes out of bounds or the referees stop the game to protect an injured player.

- **Inform your table co-officials of** how many seconds are left before each throw-in (e.g. 6 seconds on the shot).

值得注意的是，有些进攻计时设备在清屏后并不停止计时。至关重要的是，进攻计时员在赛前检查设备时必须确认其设备是否具备此特性。这可以避免进攻计时钟在诸如罚球等情况下（应当清屏期间）出现误响的可能。

如果进攻计时钟清屏需要花费太长时间以至于无法及时应用规则，那就必须放弃使用清屏功能。在这种情况下，应当按照上文所述的进攻计时钟不能清屏的情况来操作。

7.5.2 工作方法总结

进攻计时员的职责要求他／她必须全神贯注于场上球的情况，尤其是在投篮的球快要离手时和球快要接触篮圈时。正因如此，在这些极端的情况下，不要害怕发出进攻计时钟信号是非常重要的。

根据国际篮联的篮球规则,进攻计时钟的信号不应停止比赛计时钟。

- 在赛前**详细地检查设备**。
- 在赛前的例行检查中和跳球前的比赛休息期间都尽可能**使自己熟悉操作方法**。
- **你必须始终将手置于操作面板上**，并接近按钮或操纵杆的位置，而不是将手放在桌子上。因为 1/10 秒就会决定投篮得分是否有效，又或者是一场比赛的胜负。
- **全体记录台人员都必须能够清晰地看到进攻计时设备。**
- **每次复位之前，特别是在最后两分钟和即时回放的情况下，记住上一个片段剩余的进攻时间**，为的是在必要时改回原时间。
- **对球保持高度关注**，特别是在尝试投篮时。
- **优秀的进攻计时员**应当能够在快速应激和自我控制之间找到平衡，以确保规则执行的准确性和及时性。
- **为了避免失误，球队控制球发生改变之前，应当保留进攻计时钟显示的时间**。为了避免疑惑，当球出界或裁判员因队员受伤而停止比赛时，应第一时间按下停止按钮。
- 在每次掷球入界时，**提醒记录台同伴**剩余的进攻时间（例如：进攻时间剩余 6 秒）。

- **Let your table co-officials know, by calling out loudly, when there are 10 second left in a shot clock period.** The timer will then count the last 5 seconds loudly (5, 4, 3... zero).

- **Let the scorer know, by calling out loudly, when substitutions or time-outs have been requested** by the team to the left of the table, for example "Time-out, Team A / red", "Subs, Team A / red".

- **The timer shall call out loud when the last 24 seconds and last 14 seconds of a quarter have been reached.**

- At the end of each quarter, when the shot clock has been switched off, the shot clock operator will inform co-officials when there are 10 seconds left in the quarter, and will then count the last 5 seconds out loud ("5, 4, 3, 2, 1, 0").

- The scorer and the shot clock operator shall collaborate for the positioning of the alternating possession arrow at the start of the game, both being focused on the first legal control on the court.

- When there are 24 (or 14) and a few tenths of seconds remaining to the end of play, if the game clock and the shot clock are bound, in order to start them simultaneously, the shot clock operator may set the device in the start position so that, when the first legal touch happens, the shot clock starts as the timer starts the game clock.

- Help the timer by positioning the team foul marker in the correct place on their side of the table.

7.5.3   SHOT CLOCK MISTAKES

The first thing to be clear is that Table Officials can only stop the game in situations specified by the rules. An error in the application of the shot clock rule is not one of those situations, unless the use of the IRS is permitted.

This is the protocol to follow once an error has happened, for example, a reset in error.

- **Turn off the shot clock displays (blank), or reset the display to 24" and stop the shot clock from operating, and start a stopwatch.** This means that in most cases the referees will notice it, stop the game, and come to the table.

  - It will be important to remember the time that was on the game clock when the error occurred. Note this on your notice paper and start the stopwatch normally used to measure the time-outs.

- 在进攻计时钟剩余 10 秒时，大声告知记录台同伴。随后计时员应大声倒计时最后的 5 秒（"5，4，3，2，1，0"）。
- 当记录台左侧的球队**请求替换或暂停时，大声告知记录员这一信息**，例如："A 队暂停、红队暂停""A 队替换、红队替换"。
- **计时员应在一节比赛进入最后的 24 秒和 14 秒时大声喊出。**
- 在一节临近结束时，当进攻计时钟被关闭后，进攻计时员应在比赛剩余 10 秒时告知记录台同伴，并大声倒计时最后的 5 秒（"5，4，3，2，1，0"）。
- 记录员和进攻计时员应合作处理开场时的交替拥有进攻箭头，两人同时监控哪支球队在场上首先合法控制了球。
- 当临近比赛结束且比赛时间刚好剩余 24 秒（或 14 秒）又多零点几秒时，如果比赛计时钟和进攻计时钟是绑定的，进攻计时员为了同时开动它们，可以将设备处于开动模式，那样的话，一旦场上出现合法接触球，进攻计时钟便可以随着计时员开动比赛计时钟而同步开动。
- 协助计时员操作放置在记录台一端靠近他 / 她的全队犯规指示器。

7.5.3 进攻计时钟的错误

必须明确的是，记录台人员只有在规则所述的特定情况下才可以停止比赛。错误地操作进攻计时钟并不属于这些特定情况，除非被准予了使用即时回放系统。

下面规定了几种发生错误，如错误地复位时的处理方法。

- **关闭进攻计时钟（清屏）或将其复位至 24 秒，停止操作进攻计时钟，换用秒表计时。**在这种情况下，裁判员很可能会察觉到异常并停止比赛来到记录台。
  - ◆ 记住发生错误时比赛计时钟显示的时间非常重要。将这些信息记录在专门的纸张上，然后使用计量暂停时间的秒表来计量进攻时间。

- If the referees do not stop the game quickly, wait until the first dead ball occurs and then attract their attention.

- If there is not an interruption of the game, the display unit shall remain blanked until the next team control (e.g. after a shot attempt, when the ball touches the ring and control is gained by either team) and then the shot clock operation shall resume as normal.

- **If the shot clock signal sounds in error** while a team has control of the ball or neither team has control of the ball, the signal shall be disregarded and the game shall continue. However, if in the judgement of a referee, the team in control of the ball has been placed at a disadvantage, the game shall be stopped, the shot clock shall be corrected, and pos session of the ball shall be awarded to that team.

7.6 INTERVALS OF PLAY AND AFTER THE GAME

7.6.1 HELP CO-OFFICIALS:

- Help the scorer to complete the scoresheet, if needed.

- Observe the players and team bench personnel and report any incidents to the referees.

- Sign the scoresheet.

◆ 如果裁判员没有在第一时间停止比赛，应等到出现下一次死球时，才发出信号吸引裁判员注意。

◆ 如果没有出现停止比赛的情况，进攻时间设备应保持清屏状态，直到出现新的球队控制球（例如：投篮的球接触篮圈后，被任一队获得控制球），然后进攻计时钟才被恢复正常操作。

● **如果**在某队控制球或没有球队控制球时**进攻计时钟信号误响**，该信号应被忽略并且比赛应继续。然而，如果根据裁判员的判断，对方队将被置于不利，裁判员应停止比赛并纠正进攻计时钟的时间，然后再将球权判给该队。

7.6 比赛休息期间和赛后

7.6.1 协助记录台同伴

● 协助记录员完成记录表的填写（如需要）。

● 在特别情况下，观察队员和球队席人员的情况，并向裁判员报告情况。

● 在记录表上签字。

第 8 章

SUPPORTING MATERIAL

支持性材料

SUPPORTING MATERIAL

BASIC BASKETBALL OFFICIATING TERMINOLOGY

To help all the stakeholders to speak the same basketball officiating language, FIBA Referee Operations has published BASIC BASKETBALL OFFICIATING TERMINOLOGY manual. It contains a glossary of terms and abbreviations used in modern basketball officiating.

It can be read and downloaded from FIBA iRef Library App.

支持性材料

基础篮球执裁术语

为了帮助所有参与者学会说同一种篮球执裁语言，国际篮联裁判员运营部发布了《基础篮球执裁术语》手册。手册中列出了当今篮球执裁所使用的术语及其缩写。

大家可以通过 FIBA iRef Library App 进行阅读和下载。

附件
APPENDIX

WHISTLE-CONTROLLED TIME SYSTEM

The whistle-controlled time system works via a radio transmitter in the belt pack worn by the referees. Attached to the belt pack is an omnidirectional microphone, which docks in the microphone adapter on the lanyard just below the whistle.

When an referee blows the whistle, the belt pack recognises the frequency of the whistle and sends a radio signal to the base station receiver that is connected to the scoreboard controller, stopping the clock at the speed of light. The timer can also stop the game clock manually by pressing the stop button on the whistle-controlled time system console.

The whistle-controlled time system not only stops the clock; it gives the timer (and the referee), the ability to restart the clock manually. Each belt pack has a restart button, so the clock can be started from the floor, if necessary.

In this way, the effective management of the game clock is shared between the referees and the timer. Measuring time-outs and intervals of play remain duties exclusive for the timer.

Procedure when using whistle-controlled time system:

Who starts the game clock?

- **Beginning of each quarter**: At the beginning of each quarter, the game clock is started by the referee and the timer. The timer shall push the green start button on the console to start the game clock.

- **Throw-in:** The referee who administers the throw-in shall push the start button on the belt pack, and the timer shall push the green start button on the console.

哨声控制计时系统

　　哨声控制计时系统通过裁判员佩戴的腰带盒内的无线电接收器工作。腰带盒上连接着一个全指向麦克风，该麦克风会被卡扣在刚好位于口哨下方的哨带位置上。

　　当一名裁判员鸣哨时，腰带盒在识别口哨的音频后，将无线电信号传输到与记录屏控制器连接的基站接收器中，从而以光速停止计时钟。计时员依然可以通过按下哨声控制计时系统操作面板上的停止键来手动停止比赛计时钟。

　　哨声控制计时系统不仅仅具备停止计时钟的功能，它也具备允许计时员（和裁判员）手动重新开动计时钟的功能。每个腰带盒上都有重新开动按钮，为的是在必要时，裁判员在场上可以开动计时钟。

　　这样的工作方式，可以使裁判员和计时员的合作实现对比赛计时钟的高效管理。计量暂停时间和比赛休息期的职责仍应由计时员独自承担。

　　使用哨声控制计时系统的程序：

由谁开动比赛计时钟？

- **一节的开始**：每一节开始时，比赛计时钟由裁判员和计时员开动。计时员应按下操作面板上绿色的开动键开启比赛计时钟。
- **掷球入界**：执行掷球入界的裁判员应按下腰带盒上的开动键，同时，计时员应按下操作面板上绿色的开动键。

- **Free-throws**: A referee shall push the start button on the belt pack, and the timer shall push the green start button on the console.

- **Last two minutes**: In the last two (2) minutes of the fourth quarter and in the last two (2) minutes of any overtime the referee who administers the throw-in shall push the start button on the belt pack, and the timer shall push the green start button on the console.

Who stops the game clock?

- **During the game:** Each sound of an referee's whistle automatically stops the game clock. When the game clock is stopped, a red LED light on the console lights up. The timer shall push the red stop button on the console at the same time as the referee blows the whistle (to ensure the game clock stops correctly).

- **Shot clock violation:** If a shot clock violation occurs when a team is in control of the ball, the timer shall push the red stop button on the console when the shot clock signal sounds.

- **Last two minutes:** In the last two (2) minutes of the fourth quarter and in the last two (2) minutes of any overtime, the timer shall push the red stop button on the console if a field goal is scored. (This is because referees do not blow their whistle when field goals are scored).

- **Field goal leading to a time-out request:** If a field goal is scored against a team which has requested a time-out, the timer shall push the red stop button on the console.

- **罚球**：一名裁判员应按下腰带盒上的开动键，同时，计时员应按下操作面板上绿色的开动键。
- **最后 2 分钟**：在第 4 节和任何决胜期的最后 2 分钟内，执行掷球入界的裁判员应按下腰带盒上的开动键，同时，计时员应按下操作面板上绿色的开动键。

由谁停止比赛计时钟？

- **比赛期间**：每一次裁判员的哨声都使比赛计时钟自动停止。当比赛计时钟停止时，操作面板上的红灯亮起。计时员应在裁判员鸣哨的同时按下操作面板上红色的停止键（以确保及时停止比赛计时钟）。
- **进攻时间违例**：如某队控制球时发生进攻时间违例，计时员应在进攻计时钟信号响时按下操作面板上红色的停止键。
- **最后 2 分钟**：在第 4 节和任何决胜期的最后 2 分钟内，如果出现球中篮情况，计时员应按下操作面板上红色的停止键（因为裁判员并不会因为球中篮而鸣哨）。

- **球中篮后准予的暂停**：如某队请求一次暂停后对方中篮得分，计时员应按下操作面板上红色的停止键。

Console reset

Every 4-5 blows of the referees' whistle, the timer shall reset the console when the game clock is stopped (red led is light on). To do this, the timer shall push the red stop button on the console.

It is important to note that if the game clock does not start for some reason (error / delay and/or malfunctioni ng), the timer shall push the green start button on the console.

In the same way, if the game clock doesn't stop for some reason, the timer shall push the red stop button on the console.

It is also important that the timer pays attention to the flashing of the transmitter LEDs. If the transmitter LEDs are flashing it means the transmitter on the referee's belt is not working properly, or is about to stop working. It is important to advise the relevant referee as soon as possible, during the next dead ball opportunity, so that the transmitter can be changed.

操作面板的重置

在每4～5声裁判员鸣哨后，计时员应在比赛计时钟停止时（红灯亮起）重置操作面板。计时员应按下操作面板上红色的停止键进行重置。

需要格外注意的是，如果比赛计时钟因一些原因而未被开动（失误、延误和/或故障），计时员应按下操作面板上绿色的开动键。

同样，如果比赛计时钟因一些原因而未被停止，计时员应按下操作面板上红色的停止键。

计时员还应特别注意接收器的 LED 是否闪光，这一点同样重要。如果接收器的 LED 出现闪光，便意味着裁判员的腰带盒没有正常工作，或即将停止工作。同样重要的是，出现这种情况后在下一次死球期间应尽快通知对应的裁判员，以便更换接收器。

NOTE:

NOTE:

NOTE:

NOTE: